National *Childcare* Strategy

Report of the Partnership 2000
Expert Working Group on Childcare

BAILE ÁTHA CLIATH
ARNA FHOILSIÚ AG OIFIG AN tSOLÁTHAIR
Le ceannach díreach ón
OIFIG DHÍOLTA FOILSEACHÁN RIALTAIS
TEACH SUN ALLIANCE, SRÁID THEACH LAIGHEAN,
BAILE ÁTHA CLIATH 2,
nó tríd an bpost ó
FOILSEACHÁN RIALTAIS, AN RANNÓG POST-TRÁCHTA,
4-5 BÓTHAR FHEARCHAIR, BAILE ÁTHA CLIATH 2
(Teil: 01 6613111 - Fo-line 4040/4045; Fax: 01 4752760)
nó tríd aondioltoir leabhar

DUBLIN
PUBLISHED BY THE STATIONERY OFFICE
To be purchased directly from the
GOVERNMENT PUBLICATIONS SALES OFFICE
SUN ALLIANCE HOUSE, MOLESWORTH STREET, DUBLIN 2
or by mail order from
GOVERNMENT PUBLICATIONS, POSTAL TRADE SECTION,
4-5 HARCOURT ROAD, DUBLIN 2
(Tel: 01 6613111 - EXT 4040/4045; Fax: 01 4752760)
or any other bookseller

£5.00
(PN No. 6747)
© Government of Ireland 1999
ISBN: 0707667208

Contents

Foreword

Executive Summary
Achoimre Feidhmiúcháin

Introduction

SECTION ONE   Background Information

SECTION TWO   Identified Issues and Concerns

FOREWORD

Partnership 2000 for Inclusion, Employment and Competitiveness, in the context of equality, provided for the establishment of an Expert Working Group on Childcare. The Expert Working Group operated under the aegis of the Department of Justice, Equality and Law Reform on foot of its responsibility for equality matters.

The working process of the Expert Working Group was guided by the "spirit" of the Partnership 2000 agreement:

- "Partnership through this national agreement involves, in particular, a shared understanding of the key mechanisms and relationships in the formulation and implementation of policy.
- The partnership process reflects inter-dependence between the partners.
- The partnership is necessary because no party can achieve its goals without a significant degree of support and commitment from others.
- Partnership is characterised by a problem-solving approach, in which various interest groups address joint problems. Partnership involves trade-offs both between and within interest groups.
- The partnership process involves different participants on various agenda items, ranging from principles of national macro-economic policy to specifics of local development.
- All Social Partners accept that the benefits of economic growth be shared by all citizens in a manner that reflects this country's commitment to social solidarity and a better quality of life for all our people."
  (Partnership 2000, Ch. 11).

This spirit enabled the Expert Working Group to work through the many tensions which arose when it became clear that devising a National Strategy for the development of the childcare sector was a complex matter.

I would like to thank all the organisations who agreed to participate in the process and in particular all the members for their time and patience. Particular thanks is due to the chairpersons of the eight policy subgroups without whose dedication the task would have proved nigh impossible.

The work of the Expert Working Group could not have run so smoothly without the excellent service provided to it by the Secretariat which was supported by Area Development Management Limited and the Centre for Social and Educational Research, DIT.

Finally, I would like to thank John O'Donoghue, T.D., Minister for Justice, Equality and Law Reform, for his personal interest in and support for the activities of the Expert Working Group.

Sylda Langford

Chairperson
EXPERT WORKING GROUP ON CHILDCARE

EXECUTIVE SUMMARY

Introduction

Childcare provision in Ireland has, until now, been left entirely to parents to arrange for themselves. **There is now a virtual crisis in childcare supply**. As female labour force participation increases, childcare places are dropping, partly because childminders are opting for alternative employment in the formal economy, partly because of the impact of the Child Care (Pre-School Services) Regulations, 1996 and partly because larger childcare centres are experiencing difficulty in recruiting and retaining qualified childcare staff.

The **Expert Working Group** was established under Partnership 2000 to develop a strategy which integrates the different strands of the current arrangements for the development and delivery of childcare and early educational services. The Group, chaired by the Department of Justice, Equality and Law Reform, had wide ranging terms of reference and over seventy members, representing the relevant Government departments, social partners, statutory bodies, non-governmental organisations and parents. The term 'childcare' (See full definition section, p.xxii) as used by the Group means services providing care and education. The large membership of the Group required a multi-level working process involving plenary sessions attended by all members, eight subgroups, each focusing on a particular issue and a steering group.

The Expert Working Group was faced with a complex and challenging task. Its terms of reference were wide ranging and multi-faceted. Among the key considerations which shaped the Expert Working Group report were:

- agreement that the needs and rights of children should be a primary consideration;

- recognition that the terms of reference of the Expert Working Group were not

directed to parents who choose to care for their own children and that the needs of such parents may require a different policy solution;

- the need to meet EU requirements for Employment Guidelines and Structural Funds;

- the desirability of building on existing structures and services for delivery of childcare services, in a cost efficient partnership approach; and

- the need to develop childcare as a legitimate business and the consequent concept of "receipted expenditure" which is fundamental to the Expert Working Group's recommendations for development of the sector.

Chapter 1 : Social Context of Childcare Provision

The Expert Working Group has examined the social context of childcare provision, ie:

- Pressure for the development of childcare has been on the national agenda for the past two decades and this is reflected in the number of national reports, legislation and initiatives since the early 1980's.

- Parents use childcare for a variety of reasons.

- Demographic, social and economic changes in Ireland, in particular the increased participation of women in the workforce, have resulted in increased demand for childcare services.

- The availability and cost of childcare and the difficulties around reconciling employment and family lives are the most significant barriers to women accessing and participating in the labour force.

- As the number of employed parents increases there is a need for a public policy to help parents reconcile employment and caring for their children in a way that ensures quality of life for children, parents and families and equality of opportunities for women.

- Childcare is one of several family-friendly policies which can ensure a stronger balance between work and family life.

- The Expert Working Group considers that such policies should not be seen solely as a 'women's issue' but should be advanced from a broader perspective to include benefits that accrue to men and children.

- The rights of children to equality of care and education are also part of the childcare debate and there has been strong recognition, both nationally and internationally, of the benefit of quality childcare for children, families and communities.

Chapter 2: Childcare in Ireland: Current Provision

Childcare provision is unco-ordinated, variable in quality and in short supply. State expenditure on childcare is largely targeted at children in need or in disadvantaged circumstances and much State expenditure arises as a by-product of other activities. Childcare services take a variety of forms including sessional services (e.g. pre-school playgroups, naíonraí, Montessori schools), full-day care (e.g. nurseries, crèches), childminders, drop-in centres and after school care.

A survey of childcare arrangements indicates that:
- 17% of all children aged 0-9 years avail of paid childcare.

- 58% of mothers in full time work avail of childcare as compared with 16% of mothers on home duties.

- the most commonly based form of childcare is a formal arrangement (sessional services and full-day care).

- childminding in the minder's home is the most common arrangement among women with paid jobs and the second most common overall.

- on average childcare prices are in the range of £44 to £71 per week for full-time care.

- the prices to parents of childcare (as a proportion of average earnings) are amongst the highest in the European Union. Average full-day care prices in Ireland are 20% of average earnings.

Chapter 3: Regulations, Training, Qualifications and Employment

The Expert Working Group has a number of concerns about the Child Care (Pre-School Services Regulations, 1996. The notification system under the Regulations is of limited effect and should be replaced by a registration system; there is confusion about the recommendations on qualifications of childcare personnel; the implementation process is not satisfactory and the Regulations seem to have had an adverse effect on the availability of childcare places.

Childcare training has developed on an ad hoc basis, resulting in a diversity of training courses and qualifications. Many childcare workers have gained skills and knowledge through experience rather than through formal training processes. The Expert Working Group proposes the development of a national framework of qualifications in childcare which could encompass formal and informal training programmes and the accreditation of prior learning.

Childcare as an occupation is generally not well paid or well regarded. The low occupational status accorded to childcare not only deters male participation in the sector, but has implications for the quality of provision. Low pay has also led to difficulties in the recruitment and retention of childcare staff. There is a wide range of pay in the sector with rates of pay being best developed where there is public funding for projects and lowest among childminders who are paid as little as £1. 50 per hour. Many community based childcare services depend on Community Employment Schemes to supply staff, as a source of income to meet running costs and to meet adult/child ratios. The Expert Working Group recommends that a Joint Labour Committee be set up for the industry.

Chapter 4: Childcare Provision in urban disadvantaged and rural areas

In urban disadvantaged areas, childcare services are constrained by lack of financial resources and lack of childcare infrastructure and support systems. Barriers include: prohibitive costs, inability of services to employ trained staff, lack of information and restrictive opening hours. In rural areas, barriers to childcare provision include isolation, transport problems, staff costs and the absence of training programmes adapted to the needs of rural provision. Urban disadvantaged and rural areas require childcare strategies and policies which recognise the diverse range of functions and obstacles which childcare services must address in these environments.

Chapter 5: The National Childcare Strategy: Guiding Principles

The Expert Working Group has agreed a statement of principles which are intended to underpin the National Childcare Strategy and guide all childcare services. There are 12 principles in total which have been organised under the following headings: (1) needs and rights of children, (2) equality of access and participation, (3) diversity, (4) partnership and (5) quality. The Expert Working Group sets the needs and rights of children as the primary consideration in the strategy of childcare.

Chapter 6: Rationale for a National Childcare Strategy.

Quality childcare benefits children, their parents, employers and communities in general. Studies show the **social benefits** of early education in children's cognitive and social development, particularly for children from disadvantaged areas. The positive impact of out of school programmes on the social and personal development of children has also been demonstrated. Quality childcare also benefits parents and the wider community and has an important role in combating family stress and social exclusion, particularly within families experiencing poverty and disadvantage. **Economic benefits** of investing in quality childcare are shown at a number of levels: social benefits to children leading to gains in human capital, increased employability of parents combating skill and labour shortages, improving the capacity, profitability and sustainability of childcare provision and job creation in the childcare sector. **Demand for childcare** is likely to increase by between 25% and 50% over the period to the year 2011. Future demand for childcare is also relevant to the national strategy.

Chapter 7 : Stimulating supply and supporting demand

The Expert Working Group recommends six supply side measures and five demand side measures which will improve the availability and affordability of childcare in Ireland. **These are interconnected measures, all of which need to be implemented as a package in order to be successful.** The concept of **receipted expenditure** features in most of these recommendations as the Expert Working Group considers it essential that childcare be brought out of the informal economy and developed as a legitimate business within the services sector.
A seven year time frame is envisaged for the development of childcare as a sustainable sector.

The recommended measures are:

SIX SUPPLY SIDE MEASURES

- Capital grants/relief for providers
  To upgrade premises to increase quality and quantity of supply

- Tax allowance for childminders
  To support private childminders in transition to formal economy

- Employment encouragement grants
  To encourage increased employment of trained childcare staff

- Tax relief for employers investing in childcare
  To support and stimulate employer involvement

- Funding for local level measures
  To develop after school and childcare networks

- Improve local authority planning guidelines
  To ensure consistency in local authority planning permissions for childcare services.

FIVE DEMAND SIDE MEASURES *

- Childcare subsidies
  To support low income families not in tax net to access quality services

- Improvements to FIS
  To support low earners who would not benefit from tax relief measures

- Increase ceilings for lone parent Payment
  To remove disincentives for lone parents earning over ceiling

- Personal Tax relief
  To support parents in tax net at standard rate based on receipts

- Remove treatment of childcare as Benefit in Kind
  To support and stimulate employer involvement

The Expert Working Group recommends local planning and national co-ordination mechanisms to deliver childcare policies. It proposes the establishment of county childcare committees, a national childcare management committee and an interdepartmental policy committee on childcare. **The County Childcare Committees** would comprise local childcare providers, the NGO/childcare sector, statutory bodies, social partners and parents. Each Committee would develop a seven year county childcare plan which would be submitted to the National Childcare Management Committee for approval.

The **National Childcare Management Committee** would support, appraise, resource and monitor the county childcare plans, co-ordinate national developments in the childcare field and inform national policy development. The Committee would reflect the same cross sector representative as the County Childcare Committees and would have independent status.

The **Department of Justice, Equality and Law Reform** would be the designated **lead department** for the National Childcare Strategy and would chair the **Interdepartmental Policy Committee on Childcare** which would act as a link between Government and the National Childcare Committees.

* These measures relate to receipted childcare expenses

Recommendations of the Expert Working Group on Childcare

The Expert Working Group believes that it is essential for Government to take a strategic role to secure high quality services which will be accessible to all children, to secure an adequate childcare workforce, and to develop the conditions which will optimise their work. The development and implementation of a National Childcare Strategy is recommended as the first step in such a process. The National Childcare Strategy should consist of a seven year integrated strategy comprising the recommendations contained in this Report.

RECOMMENDATION 1 (p.24):
- The present system of notification should be developed and lead to an amendment of the Child Care Act, 1991, which would provide for a system of registration of facilities and childcare workers.
- All those providing childcare services for one or more children, in addition to their own, including persons employed by the parent/s of the child, either in the child's home or in the childminder's home, should be required to register.
- Relatives (parent, grandparent, siblings, uncles, aunts and step-parents) and guardians or foster parents should be exempt from the requirement to register.
- All childcare providers who offer services to children aged 0 to 12, as defined by the Expert Working Group on Childcare, should be obliged to register under the proposed system of registration.

RECOMMENDATION 2 (p.26):
The existing notification system and the proposed system of registration should require adherence to national minimum standards, encouraging 'best practice' which will be developed in consultation and partnership with the NGO sector.

A common induction and training programme should be provided for inspection teams to ensure that there is standardisation of implementation

In addition, it is recommended that one member of the inspection team should be trained in the area of Early Childhood Care and Education.

RECOMMENDATION 3 (p.27):
A Garda clearance procedure at central level, which communicates effectively with local levels, should be put in place to provide clearance information in respect of all personnel working in childcare in whatever capacity.

RECOMMENDATION 4 (p.29):
- An occupational profile (such as the model in Appendix 3.2) and appropriate qualifications should be agreed by the proposed National Childcare Management Committee within 12 months.
- A national framework for qualifications in childcare should be developed in consultation with the proposed National Childcare Management Committee.
- The national qualifications framework for childcare should provide progressive pathways of awards, which can be achieved through formal and informal education and training programmes or through the accreditation of prior learning.
- The future development of the childcare sector should aim to achieve the following target:

  A minimum of 60% of staff working directly with children in collective services should have a grant eligible basic training of at least three years at a post-18 level, which incorporates both the theory and practice of pedagogy and child development. All training should be modular. All staff in services (both collective and family day care) who are not trained to this level should have right of access to such training including on an in-service basis.(Target 26 of the European Commission Network on Childcare action programme-Quality Targets in Services of Young Children, 1996).

RECOMMENDATION 5 (p.30):

The Expert Working Group considers it desirable that children should have contact with both men and women in childcare services and that the childcare sector should aim to achieve the following target:

Twenty per cent of staff employed in child-care in collective services should be men (Target 29 of the European Commission's Network on Childcare action programme, Quality Targets in Services for Young Children, 1996). Measures for achieving this should be examined by the National Childcare Management Committee.

RECOMMENDATION 6 (p.30):

Employment procedures should be guided by the following target:

Services should adopt employment procedures which emphasise the importance of recruiting employees who reflect the ethnic diversity of the local community (Target 36 of the European Commission Network on Childcare Quality Targets in Services for Young Children, 1996).

RECOMMENDATION 7 (p.32):

A national pay scale should be established to reflect the social and economic value of the work undertaken by childcare workers. The mechanism proposed is a Joint Labour Committee (JLC) which will be required to set a JLC rate for the industry.

RECOMMENDATION 8 (p.33):

- FÁS should prioritise its Community Employment resources towards providing a dedicated childcare training and work experience initiative.
- FÁS should continue to develop childcare training initiatives within Community Employment in consultation with the National Childcare Management Committee.
- The proposed National Childcare Management Committee should explore and support the development of other routes for those who wish to work in the childcare sector.

RECOMMENDATION 9 (P.40):

Within the National Childcare Strategy, the needs of children and families experiencing poverty, disadvantage or social exclusion should be prioritised and resources targeted accordingly.

RECOMMENDATION 10 (p. 59):

- The Equal Opportunities Childcare Programme should be expanded so that the supply of quality childcare in disadvantaged areas can continue to be physically upgraded and have enhanced staffing support.
- An additional £3.5m budget should be allocated to the Programme for each of the first three years of the National Childcare Strategy.

RECOMMENDATION 11 (p.59):

Enhanced capital allowances should be provided to group-based childcare services/businesses.

RECOMMENDATION 12 (p.59):

- A new grant scheme should be established for small scale private providers and self-employed childminders not eligible for other supports, towards the capital upgrading of premises to comply with the Child Care (Pre-School Services) Regulations, 1996.
- This scheme would operate through the Department of Justice, Equality and Law Reform.
- A budget of £2 million should be allocated in 1999 in order to respond immediately to the demand.

RECOMMENDATION 13 (p.60):

- A special tax allowance in respect of childminding earnings should be provided.
- Childminding income should be disregarded when eligibility is being determined for social welfare and ancillary benefits, for example, medical cards.
- These measures would be subject to review after three years.

RECOMMENDATION 14 (p.61):

- Employment grants of up to £5,000 for each additional new staff member employed in private and community childcare facilities, including social economy initiatives, to be operated through County Enterprise Boards.
- A budget of £5m per annum should be devoted to this purpose which would be ringfenced specifically for childcare.

RECOMMENDATION 15 (p.62):

- Employers should be allowed to offset in their tax returns expenditure incurred in relation to childcare for their employees.This expenditure could take the form of provision of childcare facilities, vouchers for childcare, or direct subsidisation of childcare places for their workers.

RECOMMENDATION 16 (p.62):

In 1999 and subsequent years, the Government should allocate £1 million:

- towards the development of after school childcare provision at local level which would include a specific training dimension, and
- towards the setting up of local childcare networks which would offer educational and training support and advice to childcare providers at local level.

RECOMMENDATION 17 (p.62):

- The Department of the Environment and Local Government, in consultation with the proposed National Childcare Management Committee, should set and publish national guidelines for the granting of planning approval for childcare facilities.
- As a matter of urgency, planning Authorities should include in their Development Plans, Planning Control Guidelines for the provision of a range of childcare facilities. These Guidelines should take account of such matters as the changing pattern of work, family structure and the range of childcare facilities that are now necessary. The Guidelines should also take account of the desirability of having such facilities located in the areas, including housing

developments, close to where the users of such facilities live.

RECOMMENDATION 18 (p.65):

- A scheme to support the childcare costs of low income parents participating in all training or education programmes provided by State agencies should be put in place, on the lines of the existing pilot scheme applicable to VTOS, Youthreach and Senior Traveller Training Programme. The subsidy would be administered by the relevant training or education authority.
- A childcare subsidy on similar lines should be also paid to parents on development and adult literacy and community education courses. The guidelines and eligibility for such subsidies should be developed by the National Childcare Management Committee, and the subsidy should be administered locally on the basis of receipted expenditure provided to the Local Childcare Committees or its agents.

RECOMMENDATION 19 (p.65):

In recognition of the value of quality childcare provision, the Expert Working Group recommends that the current practice of subsidising childcare for disadvantaged children under the current Supplementary Welfare Allowance Scheme be broadened to enable parents, who cannot afford childcare and who are undergoing training and do not qualify for any of the above subsidies, to purchase childcare places for their children.

RECOMMENDATION 20 (p.66):

The specified income limit for Family Income Supplement should be raised on a case by case basis where families incur receipted childcare costs.

RECOMMENDATION 21 (p.67):

The One Parent Family Payment scheme should be expanded to increase the ceiling of earnings to £16,000 on a case by case basis where lone parents incur receipted childcare costs.

RECOMMENDATION 22 (p.68):

A tax relief measure at the standard rate is proposed which would grant:
- relief on receipted childcare expenses of up to £4,000 per child to all family units in respect to children aged 0 to 12 years.
- allowances in respect of each child, with the allowance for first child under 5 years at £4,000 per annum, and subsequent children at £3,200.
- allowances for children 5 years and over (school going children) at £2,000 per annum.

RECOMMENDATION 23 (p.69):

Free or subsidised workplace childcare should no longer be treated as benefit in kind for income taxation purposes.

RECOMMENDATION 24 (p.70):

If a tax credit system is introduced, the Expert Working Group's recommendations in relation to tax, FIS and other demand side subsidies should be replaced by Refundable Tax Credits.

RECOMMENDATION 25 (p.75):
- County Childcare Committees, consisting of representatives from all the relevant cross sector local stakeholders be established.
- The primary focus of the Committees would be the development, implementation and monitoring of a seven year County Childcare Plan.
- The County Childcare Committee should co-ordinate the new and existing services within the area and monitor implementation of the Plan against agreed targets, which should be set by all the stakeholders.
- A budget of £2million should be allocated for the establishment, development and implementation of county structures.

RECOMMENDATION 26. (p.76):
- A National Childcare Management Committee be established with the same cross sector representation as the County Childcare Committees.

- The key objective of the Committee would be to support, appraise, resource and monitor County Childcare Plans in addition to the co-ordination of existing national developments in the childcare field, and informing national policy development.
- A budget of £0.5 million should be allocated for 1999 for the establishment, research and development costs of the National Childcare Management Committee.
- A budget of £0.5 million should be allocated for 1999 for national/regional childcare organisations of a voluntary nature, who can demonstrate a capacity to support the implementation of the National Childcare Strategy.

RECOMMENDATION 27 (p.76):
- The Department of Justice, Equality and Law Reform, should be the designated Lead Department with respect to the National Strategy for Childcare.
- This remit would be to facilitate the co-ordination of the range of childcare services across departments, to strengthen and enhance the interface between all departments with a direct and indirect role in childcare.
- An Interdepartmental Policy Committee on Childcare be established which will operate as a link between Cabinet and the National Childcare Management Committee.
- The Interdepartmental Policy Committee should also consider the recommendations of other relevant reports including the Report of the Commission on the Family (1998) and the Report on the National Forum for Early Childhood Education (1998).

Achoimre Feidhmiúcháin

Réamhrá

Go dtí seo, fágadh soláthar chúram leanaí in Éirinn faoi na tuismitheoirí, go huile is go hiomlán. **D'fhéadfá a rá go bhfuil géarchéim anois ann i dtaca le soláthar chúram leanaí de**. Ar na cúiseanna atá leis sin tá méadú ar lucht saothair ar mná iad, malairt fostaíochta á lorg ag feighlithe leanaí sa gheilleagar foirmiúil, an éifeacht a bhí ag na Rialúcháin um Chúram Leanaí (Réamhscoile), 1996, agus deacrachtaí a bheith ag mórionaid chúram leanaí foirne cáilithe chúram leanaí a earcú agus a choinneáil.

Bunaíodh an **Sainghrúpa Oibre** faoi Chomhpháirtíocht 2000 chun straitéis a fhorbairt a dhéanfadh comhtháthú ar na codanna difriúla a bhaineann faoi láthair le forbairt agus le soláthar chúram leanaí agus sheirbhísí luathoideachais. Feidhmíonn an Grúpa faoin Roinn Dlí agus Cirt, Comhionannais agus Athchóirithe Dlí (cathaoirleach); tá téarmaí leathana tagartha aige agus breis is seachtó ball. Tá ionadaíocht ann ag na ranna Rialtais cuí, na compháirtithe sóisialta, comhlachtaí reachtúla, eagraíochtaí neamhrialtais agus tuismitheoirí. Baineann an Grúpa feidhm as an téarma 'cúram leanaí' chun seirbhísí cúraim agus oideachais a chur i gcéill. Toisc ballraíocht mhór a bheith ag an nGrúpa bhí gá le próiseas oibre il-leibhéil ina raibh seisiúin iomlánacha agus na baill i láthair, ocht bhfoghrúpa agus a chúram féin orthu go léir agus grúpa stiúrtha.

Ba chasta agus ba dhúshlánach an tasc a bhí le déanamh ag an Saingrúpa Oibre. Ba leathan agus ba ilghnéitheach iad na téarmaí tagartha aige. I measc na bpríomhnithe a mhúnlaigh tuairisc an tSainghrúpa Oibre bhí:

- gur aontaíodh go gcaithfí tús áite a thabhairt do riachtanais agus do chearta leanaí;

- go n-aithneofaí nach dírithe ar thuismitheoirí a thugann aire dá bpáistí féin iad téarmaí tagartha an tSainghrúpa Oibre agus go bhféadfadh réiteach polasaí eile a bheith de dhíth ar na tuismitheoirí sin;

- gur gá teacht le forálacha an AE maidir le Treoirlínte Fostaíochta agus cistí struchtúracha;

- go mba inmhianaithe é tógáil ar na struchtúir atá ann cheana chun seirbhísí chúram leanaí a chur ar fáil agus sin ar bhonn na comhpháirtíochta costéifeachtaí; agus

- an gá atá le cúram leanaí a fhorbairt mar ghnó dlisteanach agus an coincheap a leanann é, is é sin "caiteachas agus admháil", bunmholadh de mholtaí an tSainghrúpa Oibre máidir le forbairt na hearnála seo.

Caibidil 1: Comhthéacs Sóisialta Chúram Leanaí

- Tá iniúchadh déanta ag an Sainghrúpa Oibre ar chomhthéacs sóisialta sholáthar chúram leanaí,

- Le scór bliain anuas tá brú ar an gclár gnó náisiúnta chun cúram leanaí a fhorbairt agus is léir sin ó líon na dtuarascálacha náisiúnta, ón reachtaíocht agus ó thionscnaimh eile ó thús na 1980.

- Baineann tuismitheoirí leas as cúram léanaí ar chúiseanna éagsúla.

- Tá éileamh breise ar sheirbhísí chúram leanaí in Éirinn de bharr athruithe déimeagrafacha, sóisialta agus eacnamaíochta go háirithe breis den bhantnacht a bheith sa lucht saothair.

- An rud is mó atá ag cur isteach ar mhná atá ag iarraidh teacht ar an lucht saothair agus a bheith páirteach ann ná infhaighteacht agus costas chúram leanaí agus na deacrachtaí a bhaineann le cúrsaí fostaíochta agus cúrsaí an teaghlaigh a thabhairt le chéile.

- De réir mar atá líon na dtuismitheoirí fostaithe ag dul i méid tá gá le polasaí poiblí a chabhródh le tuismitheoirí chun fostaíocht agus cúram leanaí a thabhairt le chéile ar shlí a dheimheodh cáilíocht na beatha do pháistí, do thuismitheoirí agus do theaghlaigh agus comhdheiseanna do mhná.

- Polasaí amháin de pholasaithe atá cairdiúil le teaghlaigh is ea cúram leanaí agus d'fhéadfadh sé cothromaíocht níos láidre a dheimhniú idir cúrsaí oibre agus cúrsaí an teaghlaigh.

- Ní dóigh leis an Sainghrúpa Oibre gur cheart féachaint ar na polasaithe sin mar "cheist do no mná" amháin; ba chóir bonn níos leithne a bheith fúthu chun na sochair a bhainfeadh fir agus páistí as a chur san áireamh.

- Cuid den díospóireacht i leith chúram leanaí is ea cearta na leanaí chun a sciar cothrom féin de chúram agus d'oideachas a fháil agus tá aitheantas tugtha go feilmeanta, ar bhonn náisiúnta agus idirnáisiúnta araon, don tairbhe a bhaineann páistí, teaghlaigh agus pobail as dea-chúram leanaí.

Caibidil 2: Cúram Leanaí in Éirinn: An Soláthar Reatha

Is neamh-chomhordaithe é soláthar chúram leanaí, ní d'aon chaighdeán amháin é agus is tearc a líon. Dírítear caiteachas an stáit i leith chúram leanaí ar pháistí atá i ngátar nó faoi mhíbhuntáiste agus eascraíonn a lán den chaiteachas sin as seachtháirge d'imeachtaí eile.

Tá saghsanna éagsúla seirbhísí chúram leanaí ann agus seirbhísí seisiúin san áireamh (mar shampla grúpaí súgartha, naíonraí, scoileanna Montessori), cúram lán lae (e.g. naíonlanna, créiseanna), feighlithe leanaí, an t-ionad buail isteach agus cúram iarscoile.

Léiríonn suirbhé a rinneadh ar shocruithe chúram leanaí:

- go bhfuil 17% de leanaí uile na tíre idir 0-9 mbliana d'aois a n-íoctar as cúram leanaí dóibh.

- baineann 58% de mháithreacha atá ag obair go lánaimseartha leas as cúram leanaí i gcomparáid le 16% de mháithreacha atá i mbun dualgas sa bhaile.

- an cineál chúram leanaí is coitianta ná socrú foirmiúil (seirbhísí seisiún agus cúram lán lae).

- an socrú is coitianta a dhéanann mná a bhíonn ag obair agus a fhaigheann íocaíocht ná an cúram leanaí ag tarlú i dteach an fheighlí agus is é sin an socrú atá sa dara háit san iomlán.

- is é an meánréimse praghsanna ná idir £44 agus £71 in aghaidh na seachtaine - cúram lánaimseartha.

- Tá na praghsanna seo (mar chodán de theacht isteach meánach) ar chuid de na praghsanna is airde san AE. Is ionann praghsanna chúram lán lae in Éirinn agus 20% den mheánioncam.

Caibidil 3: Rialúcháin, Oiliúint, Cáilíochtaí agus Fostaíocht

Bheadh roinnt ceisteanna ag an Sainghrúpa Oibre i dtaobh na Rialúchán um Sheirbhísí Chúram Leanaí (Réamhscoile), 1996. Ní lánéifeachtach é an córas fógra atá ag feidhmiú faoi na Rialúcháin agus ba chóir córas cláraithe a chur ina áit; tá mearbhall ag baint leis na moltaí a thagraíonn do cháilíochtaí phearsanra chúram leanaí, ní sásúil é an córas cur i ngníomh agus dhealródh sé gur toradh diúltach a bhí ar na Rialúcháin i dtaca le hinfhaighteacht ionaid chúram leanaí de.

Is ar bhonn ad hoc a forbraíodh oiliúint chúram leanaí agus dá dheasca sin is iomaí saghas cúrsa oiliúna agus cáilíochta atá ann. Tá go leor oibrithe chúram leanaí ann a bhfuil scileanna agus eolas acu a fuaireadar trí thaithí seachas trí phróisis fhoirmiúla oiliúna. Molann an Sainghrúpa Oibre go gcuirfí frámaíocht náisiúnta cáilíochtaí sa chúram leanaí ar bun a chuimseodh cláir oiliúna ar bhonn foirmiúil agus neamhfhoirmiúil araon agus creidiúnú i dtaca le foghlaim roimhe sin de.

Gairm is ea an cúram leanaí nach bhfuil ardmheas air agus ní íoctar na hoibrithe go maith. Baineann stádas íseal gairme le cúram leanaí agus seachnaíonn fir an earnáil seo; tá impleachtaí ansin maidir le cáilíocht an tsoláthair. Cúis eile a mbíonn deacrachtaí ann maidir le foirne chúram leanaí a earcú agus a choinneáil is ea pá íseal. Tá réimse leathan pá san earnáil seo agus baineann na rátaí is fearr leis na tionscadail sin a fhaigheann airgeadú poiblí agus é chomh híseal le £1.50 san uair in áiteanna eile. Bíonn go leor seirbhísí pobail san earnáil seo ag brath ar Scéimeanna Fostaíochta Pobail chun foireann a sholáthar, mar fhoinse ioncaim chun déileáil le costais reatha agus chun teacht leis an gcóimheas aosach/leanaí a mholtar. Molann an Sainghrúpa Oibre go mbunófaí Comhchoiste Saothair don tionscal seo.

Caibidil 4: Soláthar Chúram Leanaí í gceantair uirbeacha faoi mhíbhuntáiste agus i gceantair faoin tuath

I gceantair uirbeacha faoi mhíbhuntáiste, bíonn bac ar sheirbhísí chúram leanaí toisc na hacmhainní airgeadais a bheith in easnamh nó bonneagar chúram leanaí agus córais tacaíochta a bheith in easnamh.I measc na mbacanna tá: costais ró-ard, na seirbhísí gan a bheith in ann foireann oilte a fhostú, easpa eolais agus uaireanta oscailte a bheith sriantach. Ar na bacanna a áirítear i gceantair faoin tuath tá: iargúltacht, fadhbanna iompair, costais foirne agus easpa clár oiliúna a oireann do thimpeallacht na tuaithe. Tá gá le straitéisí agus le polasaithe i leith chúram leanaí a d'aithneodh an réimse éagsúil feidhmeanna agus bacanna is gá do na seirbhísí chúram leanaí díriú orthu sna

ceantair uirbeacha faoi mhíbhuntáiste agus i gceantair faoin tuath faoi seach.

Caibidil 5: Straitéis Náisiúnta i leith Chúram Leanaí: Treoirphrionsabail

Tá an Sainghrúpa Oibre aontaithe sa ráiteas prionsabal a bheadh mar bhonn le Straitéis Náisiúnta i leith Chúram Leanaí agus mar threoir do na seirbhísí chúram leanaí go léir. 12 prionsabal ar fad atá ann agus iad eagraithe faoi na ceannteidil a leanas: (1) riachtanais agus cearta leanaí, (2) infhaighteacht agus rannpháirtíocht ar bhonn cothrom, (3) éagsúlacht, (4) comhpháirtíocht agus (5) caighdeán ard. An gad is gaire don scornach, dar leis an Sainghrúpa Oibre, ná straitéis i leith chúram leanaí a bheith bunaithe ar riachtanais agus ar chearta leanaí.

Caibidil 6: Réasúnú i leith Straitéis Náisiúnta um Chúram Leanaí

Baineann páistí, a dtuismitheoirí, fostóirí agus an pobal i gcoitinne tairbhe as cúram leanaí den scoth. Léiríonn staidéir na **buntáistí sóisialta** a bhaineann le luathoideachas maidir le forbairt chognaíoch agus forbairt shóisialta an linbh, go háirithe leanaí ó cheantair faoi mhíbhuntáiste. Léiríodh freisin an tionchar dearfach a bhíonn ag cláir lasmuigh den scoil ar fhorbairt phearsanta agus ar fhorbairt shóisialta an linbh. Baineann tuismitheoirí agus an pobal i gcoitinne leas as cúram leanaí den scoth agus tá ról tábhachtach aige mar le dul i ngleic le strus teaghlaigh agus eisiamh sóisialta, go háirithe an teaghlach atá i ngleic le bochtaineacht agus le míbhuntáiste. Léirítear na **buntáistí eacnamaíocha** a éiríonn as infheistiú i gcúram leanaí den scoth ar roinnt leibhéal: buntáistí sóisialta ag páistí as a dtagann breis chaipitil dhaonna, fostaíocht bhreise do thuismitheoirí a théann i ngleic le ganntanas scileanna agus lucht saothair, feabhas ar chumas, ar bhrabúsacht agus ar chothbháil sholáthar chúram leanaí agus cruthú jabanna san earnáil chúram leanaí. Is dócha go mbeidh ardú ar an **éileamh ar chúram** leanaí de 25% go 50% as seo go dtí an bhliain 2011. Baineann an t-éileamh seo a shamhlaítear leis an straitéis náisiúnta chomh maith.

Caibidil 7: Soláthar a spreagadh agus tacú le héileamh

Molann an Sainghrúpa Oibre sé cinn de sheach-chéimeanna soláthair agus cúig cinn de sheach-chéimeanna éilimh a chuirfidh feabhas ar infhaighteacht agus ar shaoire chúram leanaí in Éirinn. **Tá na céimeanna seo fite fuaite ina chéile, agus ní mór iad go léir a chur i bhfeidhm mar phacáiste chun go n-éireodh leo.** Mar chuid de na moltaí seo go léir, nach mór, tá coincheap iontu de **chaiteachas agus admháil** agus is den riachtanas é dar leis an Sainghrúpa Oibre cúram leanaí a bhaint amach as an ngeilleagar neamhfhoirmiúil agus é a fhorbairt mar ghnó dlisteanach laistigh d'earnáil na seirbhísí.

Samhlaítear frámaíocht ama seacht mbliana chun forbairt a dhéanamh ar chúram leanaí mar earnáil inmharthana.

Is iad na céimeanna atá á moladh ná:

Sé Sheach-Chéim Soláthair

- Deontais chaptitil/faoiseamh do sholáthróirí
  Áitreabh a uasghrádú chun an caighdeán a ardú agus cainníocht an tsoláthair.

- Liúntas Cánach d'Fheighlithe Leanaí
  Tacú le feighlithe leanaí príobháideacha aistriú go dtí an geilleagar foirmiúil

- Deontais chun Fostaíocht a Spreagadh
  Spreagadh a thabhairt chun go bhfostófaí níos mó foirne oilte chúram leanaí

- Faoiseamh Cánach d'fhostóirí a infheistíonn i gcúram leanaí
  Rannpháirtíocht an fhostóra a neartú agus a ghríosú.

Baineann na bearta seo le costais chúram leanaí le hadmhalacha

- Maoiniú do bhearta ar leibheál áitiúil
  Líonraí iarscoile agus chúram leanaí

- Feabhsú ar threoirlínte pleanála an údaráis áitiúil
  Seasmacht a dheimhniú ó na húdaráis áitiúla maidir le ceadanna pleanála i leith sheirbhísí chúram leanaí.

Cúig Sheach-Chéim Éilimh

- Fóirdheontais Chúram Leanaí
  Chun tacú le teaghlaigh ar ioncam íseal agus nach bhfuil sa líon cánach le go mbeadh teacht acu ar sheirbhísí d'ardchaighdeán.

- Feabhsuithe ar Fhorlíonadh ar Ioncam Teaghlaigh
  Tacú leo siúd ar ioncam íseal nach mbaineann leas as bearta faoisimh chánach.

- Buaicíocaíochtaí le Tuismitheoirí Aonair a mhéadú
  An dídhreasacht a bhaint mar le tuismitheoirí aonair a thuilleann níos mó ná an bhuaicíocaíocht

- Faoiseamh Cánach Pearsanta
  Tacú le tuismitheoirí sa líon Cánach ar ráta Caighdeánach bunaithe ar admhálacha.

- Gan déileáil le cúram leanaí mar slá
  Rannpháirtíocht an fhostóra a neartú agus a ghríosú.

Caibidil 8: Pleanáil Áitiúil agus Comhordú Náisiúnta

Molann an Sainghrúpa Oibre do na meicníochtaí sin a bhíonn ag plé le pleanáil áitiúil agus comhordú náisiúnta polasaithe chúram leanaí a chur ar fáil. Molann sé go mbunófaí coistí chúram leanaí ar bhonn contae, coiste bainisteoireachta náisiúnta ar chúram leanaí agus coiste polasaí idir-ranna ar chúram leanaí. Is é a bheadh sna **Coistí Contae um Chúram Leanaí** ná soláthróirí áitiúla chúram leanaí, an earnáil chúram leanaí/NGO, comhlachtaí reachtúla, na comhpháirtithe sóisialta agus tuismitheoirí. Dhéanfadh gach coiste plean chúram leanaí seacht mbliana don chontae a fhorbairt a chuirfí faoi bhráid an Choiste Bhainisteoireachta Náisiúnta um Chúram Leanaí le faomhadh.

Dhéanfadh an **Coiste Bainisteoireachta Náisiúnta um Chúram Leanaí** measúnú ar na pleananna chúram leanaí don chontae, tacú leo, iad a acmhainniú agus monatóireacht a dhéanamh orthu, chomh maith le forbairtí náisiúnta sa réimse chúram leanaí a chomhordú agus faisnéis a chur ar fáil ar mhaithe le forbairt an pholasaí náisiúnta. Bheadh an Coiste ag teacht leis an ionadaíocht trasearnálach ar na Coistí Contae um Chúram Leanaí agus bheadh stádas neamhspleách aige.

D'ainmneofaí an **Roinn Dlí agus Cirt, Comhionannais agus Athchóirithe Dlí mar phríomhroinn** maidir leis an Straitéis Náisiúnta um Chúram Leanaí agus is í a dhéanfadh cathaoirleacht ar an **gCoiste Polasaí Idir-Ranna um Chúram Leanaí** a bheadh ina nasc idir an Rialtas agus na Coistí Náisiúnta um Chúram Leanaí.

Moltaí an tSainghrúpa Oibre i leith Chúram Leanaí

Measann an Sainghrúpa Oibre gur den riachtanas é ról straitéiseach a bheith ag an Rialtas chun seirbhísí d'ardchaighdeán a dheimhniú agus fáil orthu ag ár gcuid leanaí go léir, i dtreo is go mbeadh líon saothair sásúil ann agus chun tosca a fhorbairt inar féidir leis an obair sin barrmhaitheas a bhaint amach. Moltar mar chéad chéim sa phróiseas sin go ndéanfaí Frámaíocht Náisiúnta um Chúram Leanaí a fhorbairt agus a chur i ngníomh. Ba cheart straitéis chomhtháite seacht mbliana, a chuimseodh moltaí na Tuarascála seo, a bheith laistiar den Fhrámaíocht Náisiúnta um Chúram Leanaí.

MOLADH 1:

- Ba chóir forbairt a dhéanamh ar an gcóras fógra atá ann faoi láthair chun go ndéanfaí leasú ar an Acht um Chúram Leanaí (1991) a chuirfeadh córas ar fáil chun áiseanna agus oibrithe chúram leanaí a chlárú.

- Is iad na daoine a chaithfeadh clárú ná iad sin go léir a chuireann seirbhísí chúram leanaí ar fáil do pháiste amháin nó níos mó, sa bhreis ar a bpáistí féin, agus san áireamh leis sin bheadh daoine atá fostaithe ag tuismitheoir/í an linbh, bíodh sé sin i dteach an linbh nó i dteach an fheighlí.

- Is iad na daoine nach mbeadh orthu clárú ná gaolta (tuismitheoir, seanathair, seanmháthair, siblíní, uncailí, aintíní agus leastuismitheoirí) agus caomhnóirí nó tuismitheoirí altrama.

- Ba chóir go mbeadh iachall ar gach soláthróir chúram leanaí a chuireann seirbhísí ar fáil do pháistí 0 - 12 bliain d'aois, mar atá sainmhínithe ag an Sainghrúpa Oibre ar Chúram Leanaí, clárú faoin gcóras clárúcháin atá á mholadh.

MOLADH 2:

Ba chóir go mbeadh an córas fógra mar atá faoi láthair agus an córas clárúcháin atá á mholadh ag teacht le híoschaighdeáin náisiúnta agus go spreagadh sé 'an cleachtas is fearr' a ndéanfaí forbairt air i gcomhar agus i gcomhpháirtíocht leis an earnáil NGO.

Ba chóir clár comónta ionduchtúcháin agus oiliúna a bheith ar fáil chun go ndeimhneodh foirne cigireachta go bhfuil caighdeánú déanta ar an gcur i ngníomh.

Anuas air sin, moltar go mbeadh traenáil faighte ag duine den fhoireann chigireachta sa réimse Luathoideachais agus Chúram Leanaí.

MOLADH 3:

Ba chóir próiseas faofa a bheith ag na Gardaí sa leibhéal láir agus a dhéanann cumarsáid éifeachtach leis an leibhéal áitiúil chun eolas a chur ar fáil faoi gach duine atá ag obair sa réimse chúram leanaí i ról ar bith.

MOLADH 4:

- Ba chóir don Choiste Bainisteoireachta Náisiúnta um Chúram Leanaí atá á mholadh aontú laistigh de 12 mí faoi phróifíl ghairme (dála na léirshamhla in Aguisín 3.2) agus faoi na cáilíochtaí cuí.

- Ba chóir Frámaíocht Náisiúnta i leith cáilíochtaí i gcúram leanaí a fhorbairt i gcomhar leis an gCoiste Bainisteoireachta Náisiúnta

- Ba chóir go gcuirfí an Frámaíocht Náisiúnta i leith cáilíochtaí i gcúram leanaí slite forásacha cáilíochtaí ar fáil agus teacht orthu trí oideachas foirmiúil nó neamhfhoirmiúil nó trí chreidiúnú a fháil ar fhoghlaim roimhe seo.

- Ba chóir an sprioc a leanas a bheith ann agus forbairt á déanamh ar an earnáil chúram leanaí:

  Ba chóir go mbeadh íosmhéid de 60% den fhoireann a bheadh ag obair go díreach le leanaí i gcomhsheirbhísí i dteideal deontais le haghadh bunoiliúna ar feadh trí bliana ar a laghad ar leibhéal iar-18, ina mbeadh teoiric agus cleachtadh na péideolaíochta agus fhorbairt an linbh. Ba cheart an oiliúint ar fad a bheith ar bhonn modúlach. Ba chóir don fhoireann go léir sna seirbhísí (comhsheirbhísí agus cúram lae teaghlaigh) nach bhfuil an leibhéal seo oiliúna orthu a bheith i dteideal na hoiliúna sin ar bhonn inseirbhíse. (Sprioc 26 de Líonra Choimisiún na hEorpa ar Spriocanna Cáilíochta Chúram Leanaí i Seirbhísí do Pháistí Óga, 1996).

MOLADH 5:

Tá an Sainghrúpa Oibre den tuairim go mbeadh sé inmhianaithe teagmháil a bheith ag leanaí le fir agus mná araon sna seirbhísí chúram leanaí agus gur chóir don earnáil chúram leanaí iarracht a dhéanamh ar an sprioc a leanas a bhaint amach:

Ba chóir gur fir a bheadh i bhfiche faoin gcéad den fhoireann atá fostaithe i gcomhsheirbhísí chúram leanaí

(Sprioc 29 de Spriocanna Cáilíochta Choimisiún na hEorpa i leith Sheirbhísí do Pháistí Óga, 1996).

Ba chóir don Choiste Bainisteoireachta Náisiúnta um Chúram Leanaí iniúchadh a dhéanamh ar na bearta is gá chun é sin a bhaint amach.

MOLADH 6:

Ba chóir an sprioc a leanas a bheith mar threoir agus nósanna imeachta fostaíochta á gcur i ngníomh:

Ba chóir do na seirbhísí glacadh le nósanna imeachta fostaíochta a chuireann an bhéim ar fhostaithe óga a earcú agus a chuireann san áireamh éagsúlacht eitneach an phobail áitiúil

(Sprioc 36 de Spriocanna Cáilíochta Choimisiún na hEorpa i leith Sheirbhísí do Pháistí Óga, 1996).

MOLADH 7:

Ba chóir scála pá náisiúnta a bhunú a bheadh ag teacht le luach sóisialta agus eacnamaíoch obair na n-oibrithe chúram leanaí. Is í an mheicníocht atá á moladh ná Comhchoiste Saothair (CS) a leagfadh ráta CS síos don tionscal.

MOLADH 8:

- Ba chóir do FÁS tosaíocht a thabhairt d'acmhainní Fhostaíocht Phobail ar mhaithe le tionscnamh taithí oibre agus oiliúna a chur ar fáil sa réimse chúram leanaí.

- Ba chóir do FÁS leanúint le forbairt na dtionscnamh oiliúna sa réimse chúram leanaí laistigh den Fhostaíocht Phobail agus i gcomhar leis an gCoiste Bainisteoireachta Náisiúnta um Chúram Leanaí.

- Ba chóir don Choiste Bainisteoireachta Náisiúnta um Chúram Leanaí atá á mholadh iniúchadh tacaíochta a dhéanamh ar bhealaí eile a fhorbairt dóibh siúd a dteastaíonn uathu a bheith ag obair san earnáil chúram leanaí.

MOLADH 9:

Laistigh den Fhrámaíocht Náisiúnta um Chúram Leanaí ba chóir tosaíocht a thabhairt do riachtanais na bpáistí agus na dteaghlach úd a dtéann an bhochtaineacht, míbhuntáiste nó eisiamh sóisialta i bhfeidhm orthu agus ba chóir acmhainní a dhíriú ina dtreo.

MOLADH 10:

- Ba chóir an Clár Comhdheiseanna Chúram Leanaí a leathnú i dtreo is gur féidir leanúint le huasghrádú fisiceach sholáthar chúram leanaí den scoth agus tacaíocht mhéadaithe ó thaobh foirne de a chur ar fáil.

- Ba chóir £3.5m a dháileadh ar an gClár agus an buiséad breise sin a bheith ann gach bliain de na trí bliana tosaigh den Straitéis Náisiúnta um Chúram Leanaí.

MOLADH 11:

Ba chóir liúntais bhreise chaipitil a chur ar fáil do sheirbhísí/ghnólachtaí chúram leanaí atá bunaithe ar ghrúpa.

MOLADH 12:

- Ba cheart Scéim Dheontas nua a bhunú do sholáthróirí príobháideacha ar scála beag agus d'fheighlithe féinfhostaithe nach bhfuil i dteideal tacaíochtaí eile, i dtreo is go ndéanfaí uasghrádú capitil ar áitreabh chun go mbeifí ag teacht leis na Rialúcháin Chúram Leanaí (Seirbhísí Réamhscoile).

- Bheadh an scéim seo ag feidhmiú tríd an Roinn Dlí agus Cirt, Comhionannais agus Athchóirithe Dlí.

- Ba chóir buiséad de £2m a dháileadh air in 1999 d'fhonn freagairt go pras don éileamh.

MOLADH 13:

- Ba chóir liúntas speisialta cánach a bheith i bhfeidhm maidir le hioncam ar fheighlíocht leanaí.

- Moltar nach n-áireofaí ioncam ar fheighlíocht leanaí agus duine á mheas le haghaidh íocaíochtaí leasa shóisialta agus sochair theagmhasacha, cárta leighis cuir i gcás.

- Dhéanfaí athbhreithniú ar na céimeanna seo tar éis trí bliana.

MOLADH 14:

- Deontais fostaíochta go dtí £5,000 do gach ball breise ar an bhfoireann a fhostaítear in áiseanna chúram leanaí, príobháideach agus ar bhonn pobail araon, agus tionscnaimh shóisialta eacnamaíocha san áireamh, iad á noibriú trí Bhoird Fiontraíochta Contae.

- Buiséad de £5m in aghaidh na bliana ar mhaithe leis an gcuspóir sin agus é dírithe go sonrach ar chúram leanaí.

MOLADH 15:

Beidh fostóirí in ann caiteachas ar chúram leanaí a bhfostaithe a dhíscríobh ar na foirmeacha cánach. D'fhéadfadh an caiteachas sin a bheith i bhfoirm áiseanna chúram leanaí a sholáthar, éarlaisí chúram leanaí nó fóirdheontas díreach le haghaidh áiteanna chúram leanaí dá n-oibrithe.

MOLADH 16:

Molann an Sainghrúpa Oibre go ndáilfeadh an Rialtas £1m in 1999 agus sna blianta ina dhiaidh sin:

- Ar fhorbairt sholáthar chúram leanaí iarscoile ar leibhéal áitiúil ina mbeadh gné shonrach oiliúna, agus

- ar líonraí aitiúla chúram leanaí a bhunú a chuirfeadh tacaíocht oideachais agus oiliúna ar fáil agus comhairle do sholáthróirí chúram leanaí ar leibhéal áitiúil.

MOLADH 17:

- Ba chóir don Roinn Comhshaoil agus Rialtais Aitiúil, i gcomhar leis an gCoiste Bainisteoireachta Náisiúnta um Chúram Leanaí atá á mholadh, treoirlínte náisiúnta a leagan síos agus a fhoilsiú maidir le faomhadh a dhéanamh agus pleanáil ar siúl le haghaidh áiseanna chúram leanaí.

- Ba chóir do na hÚdaráis Phleanála féachaint chuige go práinneach go mbeadh Treoirlínte i leith Rialú Pleanála, mar chuid dá bPleananna Forbartha, ar mhaithe le réimse áiseanna chúram leanaí a chur ar fáil. Ba chóir do na Treoirlínte sin nithe a chur san áireamh ar nós patrún na hoibre a bheith ag athrú, struchtúr an teaghlaigh, agus an réimse áiseanna chúram leanaí a bhfuil gá leo anois. Ba chóir do na Treoirlínte a chur san áireamh chomh maith a inmhianaithe is a bheadh sé na háiseanna sin a bheith lonnaithe i gceantair atá gar do lucht úsáidte na n-áiseanna sin, eastáit tithíochta san áireamh.

MOLADH 18:

- Ba chóir scéim a chur i bhfeidhm chun tacú le costais chúram leanaí i gcás tuismitheoirí ar ioncam íseal atá páirteach i ngach clár oiliúna nó oideachais a chuireann áisíneachtaí Stáit ar fáil, dála na scéimeanna píolóiteacha atá ag feidhmiú cheana i gcás VTOS, Youthreach agus an Clár Oiliúna don Lucht Taistil Sinsearach. An t-údarás oiliúna nó oideachais cuí a riarfadh an fóirdheontas.

- Ba chóir fóirdheontas chúram leanaí ar an dul céanna a íoc le tuismitheoirí atá páirteach i gcúrsa forbartha agus litearthachta d'aosaigh agus oideachais phobail. Ba chóir don Choiste Bainisteoireachta Náisiúnta um Chúram Leanaí na Treoirlínte le haghaidh na bhfóirdheontas sin a fhorbairt agus cé a bheadh i dteideal dóibh, agus an fóirdheontas á dháileadh go háitiúil ar bhonn caiteachais le hadmháil a chuirfeadh na Coistí Áitiúla Chúram Leanaí nó a ngníomhairí ar fáil.

MOLADH 19:

Chun aitheantas a thabhairt don luach a bhaineann le dea-chúram leanaí a sholáthar, molann an Sainghrúpa Oibre go ndéanfaí leathnú ar an nós atá ann faoi láthair cúram leanaí faoi mhíbhuntáiste a bheith ag teacht faoin Scéim Liúntas Leasa Forlíontach chun cur ar chumas na dtuismitheoirí sin nach acmhainn leo íoc as cúram leanaí, agus atá i mbun oiliúna agus nach bhfuil i dteideal na bhfóirdheontas thuas, áiteanna chúram leanaí a cheannach dá gclann.

MOLADH 20:

Ba chóir an teorainn ioncaim shonraithe i gcás Fhorlíonadh ar Ioncam Teaghlaigh a bheith ardaithe, ag féachaint ar gach cás ar leith ina bhfuil costais á n-íoc, agus admhálacha leo, ag teaghlaigh ar chúram leanaí.

MOLADH 21:

Moltar go leanfaí leis an scéim Tacaíocht Teaghlaigh an Tuismitheora Aonair agus go ndéanfaí leathnú uirthi chun an buaicioncam de £16,000 a mhéadú, ag féachaint ar gach cás ar leith ina mbeadh costais le hadmhálacha á n-íoc ag tuismitheoir aonair i leith chúram leanaí.

MOLADH 22:

Moltar beart faoisimh chánach ar an ráta caighdeánach a thabharfadh:

- faoiseamh ar chaiteachas ar chúram leanaí, le hadmhálacha, suas go dtí £4,000 in aghaidh an pháiste do gach aonad teaghlaigh i dtaca le leanaí idir 0 agus 12 bliain d'aois de.

- liúntas i dtaca le gach páiste de, an líuntas don chéad leanbh faoi 5 bliana ar £4,000 in aghaidh na bliana agus £3,200 i gcás gach páiste eile.

- liúntas do pháistí 5 bliana agus os a chionn (páistí scoile) ar £2,000 in aghaidh na bliana.

MOLADH 23:

Ná meastar cúram leanaí sa láthair oibre feasta - pé acu saor in aisce nó le fóirdheontas - mar shochar le hábhar maidir le cúrsaí cánach.

MOLADH 24:

- Má chuirtear córas chreidmheas cánach ar fáil ba chóir Creidmheasanna Cánach In-aisíoctha a chur in áit mholtaí an tSainghrúpa Oibre maidir le cáin FIT agus fóirdheontais láithreán éilimh eile nach iad.

MOLADH 25:

- Go mbunófaí Coistí Contae um Chúram Leanaí ar a mbeadh ionadaithe ó na coimeádaithe geallta áitiúla cuí trasearnálacha go léir.

- Príomhfhócas na gCoistí ná forbairt, feidhmiú agus monatóireacht a dhéanamh ar Phlean Chúram Leanaí 7 mBliana don Chontae.

- Ba chóir don Choiste Contae um Chúram Leanaí na seirbhísí atá ann faoi láthair agus na seirbhísí nua a chomhordú laistigh den cheantar agus feidhmiú an Phlean a iniúchadh ar bhonn monatóireachta agus na spriocanna a bheith ar aigne i gcónaí, spriocanna a leagfaidh síos na coimeádaithe geallta go léir eatarthu.

- Ba chóir buiséad de £2m a dháileadh ar mhaithe le struchtúir chontae a bhunú a fhorbairt agus a chur i ngníomh.

MOLADH 26:

- Go mbunófaí Coiste Bainisteoireachta Náisiúnta um Chúram Leanaí agus an ionadaíocht chéanna thrasearnálach is a bheadh ar na Coistí Contae um Chúram Leanaí.

- Príomhfheidhm an Choiste ná tacú le Pleananna Chúram Leanaí na gContaetha, iad a mheas is a acmhainniú agus monatóireacht a dhéanamh orthu chomh maith le comhordú a dhéanamh ar a bhfuil

d'fhorbairtí náisiúnta cheana féin ar an réimse chúram leanaí agus faisnéis a chur ar fáil ar mhaithe le forbairt ar pholasaí náisiúnta.

- Ba chóir buiséad de £0.5m. a dháileadh in 1999 ar chostais bhunú, thaighde agus fhorbairt an Choiste Bhainisteoireachta Náisiúnta um Chúram Leanaí.

- Ba chóir buiséad de £0.5m a dháileadh in 1999 ar eagraíochtaí náisiúnta/réigiúnda chúram leanaí a fheidhmíonn ar bhonn deonach agus a chruthaíonn go bhfuil siad in ann tacú le cur i bhfeidhm na Frámaíochta Náisiúnta um Chúram Leanaí.

MOLADH 27:

- Ba chóir go n-ainmneofaí an Roinn Dlí agus Cirt, Comhionannais agus Athchóirithe Dlí mar Phríomh-Roinn maidir leis an bhFrámaíocht Náisiúnta um Chúram Leanaí.

- Is é an dualgas a bheadh uirthi comhordú a dhéanamh ar réimse na Rann atá ann cheana, an comhéadan idir na Ranna go léir a neartú agus a mhéadú, na Ranna sin a bhfuil ról díreach nó indíreach acu i leith chúram leanaí.

- Go mbunófaí Coiste Polasaí Idir-Ranna a d'fheidhmeodh mar nasc idir an Chomh-Aireacht agus an Coiste Bainisteoireachta Náisiúnta um Chúram Leanaí.

- Ba chóir don Choiste Polasaí Idir-Ranna machnamh a dhéanamh chomh maith ar na moltaí a fuarthas ó Thuarascálacha ábhartha eile chomh maith leis an Tuarascáil Dheiridh ó Choimisiún an Teaghlaigh (1998) agus an Tuarascáil ar Fhóram Náisiúnta an Luathoideachais Óige (1998).

INTRODUCTION

Why Ireland needs a Childcare Strategy

The approach taken to childcare in Ireland up to now has been to leave it almost exclusively to parents to arrange for themselves. This approach worked while we had a high rate of unemployment and while the majority of women opted to leave the workforce to care for their own children.

Changed social and economic conditions and expectations have resulted in more women opting to combine work and family responsibilities at a time when the availability of childminders and places in childcare centres are contracting. The bulk of childminding has been carried out in the informal economy, mainly by women who left the workforce to care for their own children. With the growth in job opportunities many of these women are opting for alternative employment in the formal economy, where they command higher rates of pay than can be earned through childminding in the informal economy. This change has resulted in a significant drop in the availability of childminders.

The second reason for the drop in the availability of places is the impact of the Child Care (Pre-School Services) Regulations, 1996, under the Child Care Act, 1991, which commenced in January 1997. Health boards have been carrying out inspections of childcare centres. Many childcare centres are not meeting the standards required under the Regulations and are opting to close rather than make the investment required. Their profit margins are often too narrow to meet the costs of increased staff ratios and of the physical improvements required. The majority of these are small scale providers who provide the service in their own home.

The third reason for the drop in places is the difficulty which the larger childcare centres are experiencing in recruiting and retaining qualified childcare staff. Childcare staff have traditionally been low paid workers and in a buoyant economy these are being attracted away from childcare to higher paid employment.

Fourthly, parents in need of childcare for babies and parents in need of childcare places on a part-time basis have difficulty accessing childcare. This is largely due to the fact that the Regulations require higher staff ratios for babies, which increases the cost for the provider. Likewise, a part-time place increases cost for the provider when the place could be allocated to a parent seeking full-time care.

Finally, many parents are not entirely happy with the quality of the childcare service they use for their children but continue to use it because of lack of alternative provision.

The interactions of the increase in the number of women with children choosing to combine work and family life with the decrease in the availability of childcare places has caused a virtual crisis in childcare. The crisis is further exacerbated in that with the improvements in the quality of childcare, the price of childcare is increasing. As a result, many women who would like to combine work and family life cannot afford to work except those in higher income groups.

Expert Working Group on Childcare

The Expert Working Group on Childcare[1] was established in July 1997 as a result of a commitment in Partnership 2000 for Inclusion, Employment and Competitiveness, to devise a national framework for the development of the childcare sector in Ireland. In placing the development of a national framework within the context of gender equality it is recognised that "childcare is clearly an important issue in promoting equality for women and especially in promoting equal opportunities in employment". (Partnership 2000, par. 5.6.)

---

[1]Throughout the report, the term 'Expert Working Group' will be used to refer to the Expert Working Group on Childcare.

The aim of the Expert Working Group, as set out in Partnership 2000, was to develop a strategy which integrates the different strands of the current arrangements for the development and delivery of childcare and early educational services.

Responsibility for chairing the Group was assigned to the Department of Justice, Equality and Law Reform and the Department also provided the Secretariat. In addition, Area Development Management Limited (ADM) provided technical, operational support and advice to the Department on the implementation of the process and the Centre for Social & Educational Research (CSER) were engaged for editorial support. While Partnership 2000 refers to the development of a national childcare framework the Expert Working Group has decided to refer to a national childcare strategy, as the word 'framework' could be interpreted as meaning the delivery mechanisms only.

Terms of Reference
The terms of reference of the Group were drawn from Partnership 2000 and were as follows:
"The Group will consider the conclusions of the Working Group on the Job Potential of Childcare, and the ESRI survey of childcare arrangements currently being undertaken on behalf of the Commission on the Family, as well as the following specific issues:

- quantification of the job potential of the childcare sector;
- implementation of Part VII of the Child Care Act, 1991, which provides for the introduction of regulations governing safety and health standards in pre-school services and accompanying guidelines;
- the establishment of a national registration system for childcarers;
- the establishment of a nationally recognised system of certification and accreditation for childcare workers providing for an appropriate minimum qualification;
- subject to the evaluation of the current

pilot project[2], the implications of the phased extension of the Early Start Programme to all areas with continuing priority being given to areas of disadvantage;
- the financing of childcare provision by a variety of means in the interest of affordable and accessible childcare."(Partnership 2000, para. 5.7).

Membership of the Expert Working Group

The Department of Justice, Equality and Law Reform decided that membership of the Expert Working Group should be as inclusive as possible, representing all the stakeholders with an interest in the development of childcare. This strategy was adopted to ensure the development of a comprehensive national strategy which would meet the needs of all children and parents and take into account the views of as many childcare interests as possible. The 80 members represented the relevant Government departments, social partners, statutory bodies, non-governmental organisations and parents. A full list of the membership can be found in Appendix 1.1.

Definition of childcare

The Expert Working Group agreed that the term 'childcare', as used by the Group would refer to services providing care and education, which are viewed by the Expert Working Group as being complementary and inseparable. This is to distinguish the use of the term from its use within the wider health sector, where the term 'Child Care Services' refers to the variety of services for children up to the age of 18 years in need of the care and protection of the State.
The following was agreed:
- the term childcare is used by the Expert Working Group to describe daycare facilities and services for pre-school children and school-going children out of school hours.

2: The Evaluation of the Early Start Programme carried out by the Educational Research Centre, Drumcondra, Dublin 9, although complete, was not made available to the Expert Working Group

• it includes services offering care, education and socialisation opportunities for children to the benefit of children, parents, employers and the wider community. Thus, services such as pre-schools, naíonraí, daycare services, crèches, playgroups, childminding and after-school groups are included, but schools (primary, secondary and special) and residential centres for children are excluded.

The Expert Working Group also agreed that the age-group to be considered would be children aged 0 to 12 years inclusive.

Submissions
The Expert Working Group sought written submissions from the public on their views as to what should be considered as essential elements in the development of a national strategy for childcare. A total of 135 were received and the common issues arising are represented below in order of frequency:

• High quality training of childcare workers is essential **34%**
• Need for State support for childcare provision **24%**
• Quality childcare provision must be available and affordable to all **16%**
• Equality of access and participation for all children **16%**
• Registration of childcare workers and facilities **16%**
• Need for co-ordination of policy **16%**
• Recognition of accredited prior learning (APL) **10%**
• Needs and rights of children must be foremost consideration **7%**
• Needs and rights of children with special needs **5%**
• Call for involvement of men in childcare services **5%**
• Employers have responsibilities in providing for childcare **5%**.

The issues raised were incorporated in the deliberations of the Expert Working Group. A complete list of the organisations and individuals who made submissions can be found in Appendix 1.2.

Working Methods
The large membership and work process required that the Expert Working Group operate at three levels. These were:
• Plenary sessions attended by all members,
• Eight subgroups, each focusing on a particular policy issue,
• A Steering Group which comprised the Chairperson, Secretariat, chairpersons of each of the subgroups, and representatives from ADM and the Department of Education and Science.

The following subgroups were established:
• Group 1 considered the financial and employment implications of an integrated approach to the provision of childcare facilities in Ireland.
• Group 2 considered the registration, training and qualifications of childcare workers.
• Group 3 considered the resourcing and sustaining of childcare within urban disadvantaged areas.
• Group 4 considered the resourcing and sustaining of childcare within rural areas.
• Group 5 considered regulations and standards.
• Group 6 considered the educational aspects of childcare services.
• Group 7 considered the needs and rights of children in relation to a national framework.
• Group 8 considered equality of access and participation in relation to a national framework.

Terms of reference and detailed objectives were agreed for each subgroup (see Appendix 1.3).

Two of the subgroups had particular links with other initiatives. Group 5 had been established by the Department of Health and Children to monitor the implementation of the Child Care (Pre-School Services) Regulations, 1996 and was incorporated into the Expert Working Group. The aim of the Early Education Subgroup (Group 6), was to co-ordinate the views of all members of the Expert Working Group in relation to early childhood education and to make these known at the National Forum for Early Childhood Education, which took place in March, 1998. A copy of the Expert Working Group's statement to the National Forum is at Appendix 1.4.

Appendix 1.5 presents a diagrammatic representation of the working methods of the Expert Working Group.

The Expert Working Group also commissioned a number of research projects, the results of which have informed this report (see Appendix 1.6).

Other developments

Contemporaneous with the work of the Expert Working Group on Childcare during 1997 and 1998, was the work of the Commission on the Family (Department of Social, Community and Family Affairs) and the National Forum for Early Childhood Education (Department of Education and Science).

Some considerations which shaped the Expert Working Group's Report

The Expert Working Group was faced with a complex and challenging task. Its terms of reference were wide-ranging and multi-faceted and its membership large. It had to address a diverse range of issues including the needs of children, the acute problem of childcare supply, affordability of childcare, regulation and standards, the number of childminders in the informal economy and the particular problems faced by urban disadvantaged and rural areas. Its large membership brought together a wealth of experience and knowledge on childcare but it also showed how disparate the perspectives on childcare can be, depending on the background of the persons concerned. For example, some members saw childcare as being essentially about enabling women to enter the labour market; others were mainly concerned with the needs of disadvantaged areas; and others saw the quality of childcare as being

the key issue. There were many complexities and tensions which needed to be addressed and difficulties to be overcome in the development of the strategy.

The Group agreed that the needs of children and their right to access quality services, regardless of their social and economic background, should be the primary consideration in the development of a National Childcare Strategy. Throughout all the deliberations of the Expert Working Group, the needs and rights of children were placed centre stage.

One of the issues which emerged for the Expert Working Group at an early stage was that of support for parents who choose to care for their own children. It recognised that the essential difference between the needs of parents who care for their own children and those who avail of childcare services is that the use of childcare necessarily involves third parties who provide a service for the parent(s) - Parents who use childcare are service users who rely on having an adequate provision of good quality service available to them at a price they can afford. The Group recognised the desirability of bringing forward measures to assist parents who work outside the home as well as measures for parents who choose to care for their own children. It considered that these were two different policy objectives, and therefore two different policy solutions should be applied. If the two situations are treated as one policy issue, e.g. by increasing child benefit for all or by universal tax credits, the impact on the development of childcare services could be negligible. Universal policies, at the level at which the Exchequer could afford them, are unlikely to result in improving either the quality or quantity of childcare services.

The Expert Working Group was, under its terms of reference, directed towards considering childcare for parents in the labour force, or trying to access the labour force. The Expert Working Group did not, therefore, extend its recommendations to parents who work in the home. Nevertheless, it should be recognised that improving the quality and quantity of childcare will also have a positive impact on parents who choose to care for their children at home since 16% of children with parents who work full-time in the home avail of paid childcare.

An important consideration which influenced the deliberations of the Expert Working Group was the need to develop a childcare strategy to meet European Employment Guidelines and Structural Fund criteria. The 1999 European Employment Guidelines call on Member States "to design, implement and promote family friendly policies, including affordable, accessible and high quality care services for children as well as parental and other leave schemes". In its comments on Ireland's National Employment Plan for 1998, in relation to childcare the EU said that "the policy focus must now shift towards a more effective implementation of the reform process". Ireland's childcare infrastructure is much weaker than that of our EU counterparts. The Expert Working Group was conscious that if a national childcare strategy is not developed the result could be criticism of Ireland's National Employment Action Plans and in addition, forfeiture of Structural Funds for 2000 - 2006 because of failure to satisfy the equal opportunity policy requirements of the regulations for structural funds under a key criterion for childcare infrastructure support.

The strategy put forward by the Expert Working Group represents a consensus of the views of the Expert Working Group. The Group sought to develop a balanced package of measures which would take into account the needs of all sectors of society and would deal with both the supply and demand sides of childcare. The Expert Working Group has developed an interdependent package of measures which it believes addresses all the dimensions of childcare in an appropriate and balanced way.

The Expert Working Group did not seek to put forward an ambitious and costly 'wish list'. It sought to develop a workable strategy which would not entail extreme costs.

The Group took the view that its strategy should build on existing structures and services. It was felt that it would not be cost-efficient to try to establish an entirely new childcare service. The Group also recognised that childcare could not be compartmentalised (e.g. as a labour market measure, an education measure or a care measure) and agreed that harnessing and co-ordinating of the services which already exist in various Government Departments, State Agencies and the voluntary sector represented the best way forward for development of the sector.

The Expert Working Group recognised that, given the multiplicity of policies and tasks involved, a childcare strategy would take some time to develop. It envisaged that the strategy would have a seven year time-span, which would coincide with the time-frame of the next National Development Plan. It believes that the structures for co-ordination and delivery of childcare at national and local levels could be brought to maturity in that time. A seven year period would be needed to develop a quality workforce. A seven year period would also be appropriate for the operation of tax incentives and schemes outlined in Chapter 7, it is envisaged that such incentives would taper off towards the end of that period.

Central to many of the measures being put forward by the Expert Working Group for the development of the childcare sector is the concept of receipted expenditure. The Group concluded that demand side supports should be tied to receipted expenditure in order to bring childcare out of the informal economy and facilitate its development as a legitimate business within the services sector and contribute to the overall quality of childcare. It was considered that this was necessary in order to give childcare workers and childminders the recognition and value they deserved in Irish society. What has been developed, therefore, is a set of interdependent measures, which must be put in place together and which the Expert Working Group considers will not work if implemented in an isolated way.

In conclusion
This report is the culmination of a lengthy consultative process which has been supported by national and international research. It presents a seven year strategy for the development of the childcare sector, including policy recommendations and the structures and mechanisms for a needs-led planning approach at county level, within a national framework. It has been developed in consultation and partnership, and proposes a shared vision for the future of childcare in Ireland.

As a society we will be failing to meet the needs of many children and parents if we fail to develop a strategy for good quality, affordable and accessible childcare. Families are the core of our society, but many of them are under pressure trying to combine work and family life. We must support them in new ways which reflect the new challenges which they face in a rapidly changing society. This Report sets out how this can best be done.

CHAPTER I

Social Context of Childcare Provision

Demographic, social and economic changes in Ireland have resulted in increased demand for childcare services. In fact, pressure for the development of childcare has been on the national agenda for the past two decades and this is reflected in the number of national reports, legislation and initiatives since the early 1980's. The focus and perspectives represented in each report largely depends on the responsibilities of the particular appointing body and include: care and protection of children at risk or disadvantaged; standards in childcare facilities; gender equity in the labour force; and the rights of the child. The major issues identified as needing further attention included: inadequacy of services, affordability, fragmentation, lack of co-ordination, need for legal requirements and standards to be established and monitored, poor pay and conditions for workers, the role of the voluntary sector, funding, tax relief on expenditure, capital outlay and training of personnel.

Contemporaneous with the work of the Expert Working Group on Childcare during 1997 and 1998, has been the work of the Commission on the Family (Department of Social, Community and Family Affairs) and the National Forum for Early Childhood Education (Department of Education and Science).

1.1
Why parents avail of childcare in Ireland
Irish parents avail of childcare for many reasons, related to their own and their children's needs. **The need for childcare transcends all sectors of Irish society, whether urban or rural, disadvantaged or non-disadvantaged.** Parents may use a childcare service in one or more of the following circumstances:

- Parent(s) wishing to avail of childcare as part of childrearing,
- Parent(s) who want their child to avail of socialisation and educational opportunities,

- Parent(s) working,
- Parent(s) seeking work e.g. attending interview,
- Parent(s) attending education or training programmes,
- Parent(s) requiring a break due to short term family crisis,
- Parents(s) needing to attend appointments,
- Parent(s) wishing to avail of leisure or social activities,
- Parent(s) under long-term stress requiring respite.

1.2
Women and work in Ireland
One of the most important factors currently influencing the demand for childcare is the increased participation of women in the workforce. Female labour force participation has risen from 34.1% in 1992 to 39.2% in 1997 (CSO 1998, a Labour Force survey). The participation rate of females, whether with or without children, continues to increase at a rate in excess of projection. Figures for the period September to November 1997 indicate a continued expansion for women, with an overall participation rate of 45.9% (CSO).

An important feature of women's participation in the labour force is the increase in participation of mothers, especially in the last decade. Figures from the 1996 Labour Force Survey indicate that 42% of younger mothers, that is, mothers with children under 15 years of age are in employment (28% full-time and 14% part-time). This compares with older mothers with children older than 15 years - 24% of whom are in employment (15% full-time and 9% part-time).

Further breakdown of these figures reveals that 29.3% of mothers with youngest child aged 2 - 4 years are in full-time work, compared with 34% of mothers with youngest child aged 0 - 24 months (see Figure 1.1). These findings are unexpected since "the traditional wisdom in Ireland has been that mothers of very young children are most likely to stay out of the labour

Fiig. 1.1. Labour Force Participation Rate of Mothers by Age of Youngest Child

Per cent in labour force

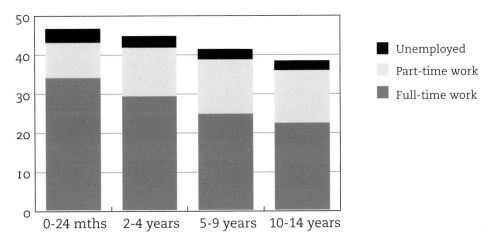

Age of youngest Child

Source: 1996 Labour Force Survey microdata files

market, while some mothers who left employment when their children were small are likely to re-enter the labour market as their children come to school going age." (Goodbody, 1998, p.20).

Part-time work represents a continuing trend amongst women in Ireland. Data and research in this area indicate that this reflects a strategy on women's part to reconcile childcare and home duties with formal employment. However, while part-time work enables women as individuals to cope, it does not solve the long-term and inter-related problems of how women can achieve formal work that is valued, skilled and decently paid while dealing with family responsibilities.

1.3 EQUAL OPPORTUNITIES

The most significant barriers which have been consistently identified as hindering greater access to and participation of Irish women in the labour force are the availability and cost of childcare and the difficulties around reconciling employment and family lives.

The responsibility for childcare still falls predominantly on women. This is the case even where both parents are present, and is even more onerous in lone parent, predominantly female headed, households. Evidence suggests that women have continued to carry out their formal working lives, while also carrying the burden of family responsibilities. As a result, women may have to compromise on standards of care, split their working day and compromise on time spent with their children. They may have to rely on traditional family support when available or accept high cost or otherwise unsuitable formal childcare.

These strategies are not equally available to all women. For example, some women have greater access to relatives than others. However, as more women enter employment the supply of relatives able and willing to provide childcare is unlikely to keep pace with increased demand. There are also inequalities between women at different income levels. High earning women can more readily afford childcare costs and have greater choice in relation to types of childcare while women at low and middle income levels may find their earnings wholly or largely absorbed by childcare costs. As the number of employed parents increases, there is a need for public policy to help parents reconcile employment and caring for their children in a way that ensures quality of life for children, parents and families and equality of opportunities for women. Gender equality is, arguably, the most influential issue affecting the area of policy in childcare at present.

The Expert Working Group on Childcare was established under Partnership 2000 in the context of promoting equality for women and especially in promoting equal opportunities in employment. Equal opportunities between women and men means ensuring that women and men can access and participate in the various 'spheres' (e.g. decision making, management), and activities (e.g. training, employment and enterprise) on an equal basis. Women and men should be equally active as participants when it is their wish to do so and should have their needs and interests equally well met.

Significant recent initiatives in relation to childcare development, which aimed to promote gender equality in the labour force and tackle social exclusion, have been led by the Department of Justice, Equality and Law Reform through Local Area Partnerships.

The Pilot Childcare Initiative (1994-1997) was an initiative which involved the expenditure of IR£2.7 million on the provision of childcare facilities in disadvantaged areas for the purpose of facilitating the participation of socially excluded mothers - or fathers where they have the main responsibility for rearing their children - in employment, training or education. The initiative was designed and managed by Area Development Management Limited (ADM). Following its evaluation, the initiative was extended in 1998 to the Equal Opportunities Childcare Programme. This programme, which has a budget of £3.6m annually, contains three funding initiatives: Capital Infrastructure Childcare Initiative, Employer Demonstration Childcare Initiative and Community Support Childcare Initiative (see also Appendix 1.8) These initiatives have done much to raise the profile of childcare and ensure its inclusion in Local Development Plans of Partnerships.

Two other initiatives of note are the New Opportunities for Women (NOW) Programme and County Enterprise Board (CEB) supported under the Operational Programme for Local, Urban and Rural Development.

The NOW Programme is a European Union programme aimed at facilitating the greater participation of women in the labour market. One of the priority issues which has been highlighted under NOW is the importance of childcare provision in ensuring that real opportunities in training, employment and self employment are accessible to women.

The Operating Agreements for CEBs require all Boards to ensure that measures supported by them comply with, and where appropriate, help to promote national and European Union policy objectives and legislation on equal opportunities for men and women. The CEBs have been concerned that women entrepreneurs are using the Boards' services to a lesser degree than their male counterparts. The European Commission has highlighted the absence of employment grants to the promoters of childcare services that are run on a sessional basis as a possible barrier to greater female participation. In January 1998, the CEBs introduced a measure whereby Boards may award employment grants on a scaled down, i.e. pro-rata basis, in respect of newly created permanent but part-time jobs (see Section 2.1 for a summary of State and European Support for Childcare).

The proposed national childcare strategy presents an opportunity to move a significant step closer to equality in the workplace by ensuring more equal access for women in training, education and employment, especially for those women who experience additional forms of discrimination and exclusion (see Chapter 4 for a more in-depth discussion of childcare in the context of urban and rural disadvantaged communities).

1.4
BALANCING FAMILY AND WORK RESPONSIBILITIES

1.4.1 Family friendly policies in the workplace

The Expert Working Group believes that balancing family and work responsibilities is about empowering women and men to have more control over their working lives and helping parents find a satisfactory balance between employment and family life. In this regard, it is important to recognise that a family's childcare needs are not static - they change over time with, for example, the birth of a second or third child or children going to school who require after school care.

Analysis carried out for the Commission on the Family on the 1996 Labour Force Survey reveals that employment among parents tends to be at a maximum when childcare duties are at their most demanding. Furthermore, it is noteworthy that in comparison to their counterparts in Europe, Irish parents work longer hours. Mothers, where they are employed, work an average of 31-32 hours per week outside the home. Fathers work an average of 46 hours per week, and a significant minority (33 per cent) work 50 hours or more per week *(Commission on the Family, 1998)*.

The current economic climate has increased the awareness amongst employers of the benefits of supporting family friendly policies, particularly childcare. The Expert Working Group acknowledges that supporting and developing childcare is just one of a range of measures which employers can adopt to ensure a stronger balance between work and family life. Other measures include job-sharing, flexible working hours, flexi-place (working from home), term time working and career breaks or sabbaticals, all of which would make the workplace more responsive to the needs of workers with children.

The 1996 Labour Force Survey shows that married women account for 50% of the female workforce and that family responsibilities were cited as by far the largest single reason for women leaving the workforce in the preceding five years (284,100 of a total of 391,300).

At present the Irish Business and Employers' Confederation (IBEC) is exploring ways to support employers' interest and involvement in childcare. The focus is primarily on finding mechanisms to respond to the growing skills shortages that are facing the business sector (see also Section 2.3.6). The Expert Working Group believes that, through family friendly policies, a response to the potential skills shortages can be addressed from the following two perspectives:

1. Attracting new employees into the labour market (specifically women with children) to meet increasing demands.
2. Retaining skilled employees (specifically women with children) in employment when childcare obstacles arise.

The business sector and employers can make a significant contribution to the development of childcare through a range of direct and indirect measures. Many employers are expressing an interest in collaborative arrangements with other employers and childcare providers, in the spirit of social partnership. There are joint opportunities emerging, which require explicit commitment and direction from employers' organisations and the trade union sector to ensure that both the economic needs of employers, and the support and social needs of the parents and children are met (see Sections 7.1.3 and 7.1.4 for further details).

1.4.2 Fathers and childcare

In the context of balancing family and work responsibilities, it is also important to recognise that the provision of quality, flexible and integrated services must be accompanied by measures to support and encourage increased involvement of fathers in the care and up-bringing of their children.

However, family friendly policies in the workplace tend to be regarded as 'women's issues' and advanced as measures to promote equal opportunities for women. Fathers and men generally are less likely to avail of them than women and mothers. In fact, fathers are not expected to behave any differently in the workplace than non-fathers.

The Expert Working Group considers that family friendly policies should be advanced from a broader perspective to include the benefits which accrue to men and children as a result of greater sharing of family responsibilities (see Section 3.3.1 for a discussion on men in childcare).

1.4.3 EU Guidelines on Employment

The European Union's philosophy is that responsibility for childcare should be shared between women and men, and between parents, employers and society as a whole. Member States are encouraged to ensure that childcare services are available for all parents who wish to avail of them. In November 1997, the European Council, in setting out employment guidelines, called on each Member State to produce a National Employment Action Plan in order that the agreed guidelines are transposed into national administrative, regulatory and other measures. The EU Guidelines were formulated within a four pillar framework:

1. Improving Employability
2. Developing Entrepreneurship
3. Encouraging Adaptability in Businesses and their Employees
4. Strengthening the Policies for Equal Opportunities.

Childcare provision contributes to the attainment of all four pillars. The benefits to parents increase employability, the benefits to employers increase adaptability, the benefits in job creation increase enterprise and the benefits to children are a cross cutting measure which permeate the other three and contribute to the attainment of an equal opportunities policy in Ireland.

1.5
PROVISIONS FOR TIME OFF WORK

One of the public supports to facilitate the reconciliation of work and family responsibilities is time off work which can take one of the following forms: maternity leave, paternity leave, adoptive leave and parental leave. Along with the U.K., Ireland has the shortest entitlement to maternity leave within the EU, matching the EU minimum statutory maternity leave of 14 weeks. There is no statutory provision for paternity leave in Ireland.

Following the EU Directive on Parental Leave, the Parental Leave Act, 1998 was implemented in Ireland on the 3rd December, 1998. This provides for a scheme of unpaid parental leave for working parents to take care of their young children. It applies to parents of children born on or after 3 June, 1996 or adopted on or after that date. Each parent has a separate entitlement to leave of up to a total of 14 weeks, for each child, which is not transferable. The leave must, in general, be taken before the child reaches the age of 5 years. The Expert Working Group notes that under the EU Directive, parental leave could apply to parents of children up to the age of 8 years.

The Parental Leave Act, 1998 also gives all employees a right to limited time off for family emergencies caused by accident or illness, known as 'force majeure' leave. This leave is paid and is separate from parental leave. It is limited to a maximum of three days in each 12 months or 5 days in each 36 month period.

The Expert Working Group welcomes the implementation of the Parental Leave Act as a first step to facilitating parents to balance work and family responsibilities. However, the Expert Working Group agrees with the view of the Commission on the Family that unless the period of parental leave is paid,

"it will not fully realise key family objectives, which include providing real opportunities to mothers and fathers in balancing their work and family responsibilities, promoting equality for working parents in the workplace and in the home in the sharing of childcare responsibilities. *(Commission on the Family, 1998, p.134)*."

1.6
THE RIGHTS OF CHILDREN TO EQUALITY OF CARE AND EDUCATION

Increasingly, the childcare debate has also focused on the rights of children to equality of care and early education. There has been growing recognition, both nationally and internationally, of the role of quality childcare services in providing enhanced social and educational opportunities for children, in addition to the substantial benefits it brings to families and communities in terms of its contribution to health, educational attainment, socialisation, participation in training and employment and job creation (see Section 6.2 for a fuller discussion around this area). The Expert Working Group agrees that the educational element of childcare needs to be explicitly addressed. This aspect of childcare is discussed in greater depth in Section 5.1.

1.7 SUMMARY

- Pressure for the development of childcare has been on the national agenda for the past two decades and this is reflected in the number of national reports, legislation and initiatives since the early 1980's.
- Irish parents avail of childcare for many reasons, related to their own and their children's needs. The need for childcare transcends all sectors of Irish society, whether urban or rural, disadvantaged or non-disadvantaged.
- Demographic, social and economic changes in Ireland have resulted in increased demand for childcare services. Of particular note is the increased participation of women in the workforce.
- An important feature of women's participation in the labour force is the increase in participation of mothers generally, and particularly mothers of very young children, especially in the last decade.
- As the number of employed parents increases, there is a need for public policy to help parents reconcile employment and caring for their children in a way that ensures quality of life for children, parents and families and equality of opportunity for women.
- The provision of quality, flexible and integrated services must be accompanied by measures to support and encourage increased involvement of fathers in the care and upbringing of their children, in addition to measures by employers and trade unions, which are supported by Government, to make the workplace more responsive to the needs of workers with children.
- The rationale for family friendly policies needs to be broadened to include the benefits which accrue to men and children as a result of greater sharing of family responsibilities.
- There has been growing recognition, both nationally and internationally, of the role of quality childcare services in providing enhanced social and educational opportunities for children, in addition to the substantial benefits it brings to families and communities in terms of its contribution to health, educational attainment, socialisation, participation in training and employment and job creation.

CHAPTER 2

Childcare in Ireland: Current Provision

Compared to other OECD and EU countries, the provision of childcare services in Ireland is limited. As in most countries, there is a wide variety of childcare services which are both centre and family-home based. However, present service provision lacks co-ordination and varies widely in quality. No Government has had a coherent approach to national childcare policy and governmental childcare initiatives over the years have been reactive rather than proactive. The Expert Working Group believes that, in 1998/99, the lack of provision of quality childcare has reached a crisis level. Many services have long waiting lists and parents have difficulty accessing information on what is available.

much of the expenditure on childcare arises as a by-product of other activities and does not have improvement in childcare provision as an objective.

2.1
STATE AND EUROPEAN SUPPORT FOR CHILDCARE

In assessing the extent to which the State and the European Union provide support to childcare services in Ireland, support provided by each of the Government departments was identified. Support which is channelled through the Operational Programmes (O.P.) for Human Resources and Local, Urban and Rural Development was also considered as was support provided under a number of EU Community Initiatives. A summary of sources of State and European Union support for childcare is presented in Table 2.1.

Overall, State expenditure is targeted largely at those children in need, in disadvantaged circumstances and/or deemed to be at risk. It has also been noted that a number of sources are sometimes used to fund different aspects of the same childcare service. Furthermore, much of the expenditure on childcare arises as a by-product of other activities, and does not have improvement in childcare provision as an objective. An example cited is the Community Employment Programme which does not have a childcare objective per se, but supports childcare through placement of trainees in social economy jobs generally (see sections 3.3.4 and 4.6 for further discussion on the Community Employment Programme).

2.2
NUMBER OF CHILDREN AVAILING OF CHILDCARE

The Survey of Childcare Arrangements[1] which was undertaken by the ESRI for the Commission on the Family (1998) is the most comprehensive and up-to date data source available with which to measure the demand for childcare in Ireland. The purpose of the survey was to provide information on the care arrangements of children and their families, focusing on the childcare services used by parents who work full-time in the home as well as those who work outside the home. From a national probability sample of 4,276 households, the survey identified 1,278 households containing children aged 12 years or under. It collected detailed information on how children in those households were cared for in the week prior to interview (the 'reference week').

For the purposes of analysis and presentation, households with children of two age groups were identified: 0 to 4 years and 5 to 9 years. The ESRI survey also provided data on children aged 10 to 12 years, but the data showed that the level of childcare usage in that age group was negligible. This may be indicative of the number of children in the age group of 10 to 12 years who care for themselves in the hours after school before parents return from work.

---

[1] The survey was carried out in the months of November and December 1996 and February 1997. In all cases, the reference week to which the data referred occurred during school term. A basic report on this survey, including an account of the methodology used is available in Chapter 19 of Strengthening Families for Life *(Commission on the Family, 1998)*. The survey did not distinguish between sessional and full day care services.

Table 2.1 Summary of Sources of State and European Union Support for Childcare

Co-ordinating Department Source	Programmes	Dominant Funding
Health & Children	Community based services provided by the health boards Support for National organisations	Exchequer
Education & Science	Vocational Training Opportunities Scheme VTOS	O. P. for Human Resource Development
	Youthreach	O. P. for Human Resource Development
	Traveller Training Programmes	O. P. for Human Resource Development
	Traveller Pre-Schools	Exchequer
	Early Start Pre-School Programme	Exchequer
Justice, Equality & Law Reform	Childcare Infrastructure Projects	Exchequer/ERDF
	National Employer Childcare Demonstration Initiative	Exchequer/ERDF
	Community Based Childcare Projects in Disadvantaged Areas	Exchequer
Arts, Heritage, Gaeltacht & the Islands	Údaras na Gaeltachta	Exchequer
	An Comhchoiste Reamhscolaíochta Teo	Exchequer
Enterprise, Trade & Employment	County Enterprise Board support	O. P. for Local, Urban and Rural Development
	NOW Programme	EU Community Initiative (Employment)
	FÁS Childcare Training	O. P. for Human Resource Development
	Community Employment Programme	Exchequer
Agriculture & Food	Capital grant expenditure	EU Community Initiative (LEADER II)
Social, Community & Family Affairs	Voluntary & Community Services Grant Schemes	Exchequer

Environment	Non-specific Local Authority projects	Exchequer
Tourism, Sport & Recreation	Non-specific projects	Exchequer
	Infrastructure projects, new initiatives and provision of staff in Partnerships & Community Groups	O. P. for Local , Urban & Rural Development
	Programme for upgrading childcare facilities	EU Community Initiative (Urban)
Finance	Subprogramme for Social Inclusion	Special Support Programme for Peace and Reconciliation
	Communities in Action	IFI
	Cross Border Rural Childcare Project	Community Initiative (Interreg II)
Taoiseach	Territorial Employment Pacts	O. P. for Local , Urban & Rural Development

The findings indicate that 38% of parents with children aged 0 to 4 years and 18% aged 5 to 9 years avail of paid childcare. When these figures are applied to the total number of children in these groups, it is estimated that 146,000, or 17% of all children between the ages of 0 to 9 years avail of paid childcare.

The survey also revealed that take-up of paid childcare varied with the employment status of the mother. Table 2.2 (p. 14) shows that only 16% of children with mothers who work full-time in the home avail of childcare, as compared to 58% of children of mothers in full-time work.

The findings indicate that 38% of parents with children aged 0 to 4 years and 18% aged 5 to 9 years avail of paid childcare

2.3
CURRENT CHILDCARE SERVICE PROVISION

Childcare provision in Ireland takes a variety of forms. For the purposes of clarity, service provision is outlined under the headings utilised by the Child Care (Pre-School Services) Regulations, 1996 (see Section 3.1) i.e. sessional services, full-day care, childminders and drop-in centres. Other categories outlined include the Early Start Programme, childcare provided by employers, after school care, and parent and toddler groups, and au pairs. In the absence of co-ordinated State support for this sector, much of the work over the last 30 years in developing, supporting and advising community childcare facilities has been the result of the commitment of volunteers (see also Section 4.4).

2.3.1 Sessional Services
Playgroups
Playgroups offer care and education, mainly on a sessional basis, to children aged 3 to 5 years. Approximately 80% of playgroups are

privately run home-based playgroups. The remainder are community based and committee managed. The IPPA, an Early Childhood Organisation established in 1969, offers training and local support and advice to parents and childcare providers.

Naíonraí

An Comhchoiste Reamhscolaíochta Teo, set up in 1978, organises and supports a system of Irish language medium playgroups, the Naíonraí. Naíonraí offer a sessional service for 3 to 5 year-old children. In June, 1998 there were 254 Naíonraí in the Republic of Ireland, 89 of which were located in Gaeltacht areas.

Montessori Schools

There are approximately 500 Montessori schools/pre-schools in Ireland registered with AMI Teacher Association and St. Nicholas Montessori Society of Ireland. These provide a part-time pre-school service for children aged 3 to 6 years using primarily the Montessori Method. In March 1998, these two organisations came together to form the Irish Montessori Education Board (IMEB) to provide an overall accreditation body for Montessori schools and teachers in Ireland.

Steiner Kindergartens

There are 12 kindergartens in Ireland registered with the Irish Steiner Kindergarten Education Association. These community based kindergartens provide holistic childcare on a sessional or full day care basis.

2.3.2 Full Day Care

Nurseries/Crèches

Nurseries provide group care for children aged from 3 months. The National Children's Nurseries Association (NCNA) was formed in 1988 to co-ordinate and bring together providers offering full day care for young children and families. In July 1998, there were approximately 400 nurseries, catering for approximately 13,000 children aged between 0 and 6 years, registered as affiliated members of NCNA. These nurseries may be private, community based or in the workplace. Many provide a formal

education component in the form of morning pre-school sessions for the 3 to 5 year olds.

A recent survey of NCNA members[2], which was undertaken as part of the Economics of Childcare Report (*Goodbody*, 1998), revealed that 80% of centres are owner managed. Just over half (50.6 %) operate from converted homes, 36.4% from other converted premises, and 13% from purpose built facilities. The average number of places per centre was 42. The great majority of children attending are cared for full-time.

The same survey indicates that there is a growing demand for places in nurseries/crèches. One third of respondents to the survey receive more than 8 queries per week for places. 96% reported that the level of queries had increased in the past year. It is interesting to note that queries in respect of places for babies pre-dominated, with part-time places being the next most frequent.

There is a number of Irish language nurseries in Gaeltacht areas. In 1998, there were three in the Connemara and Aran Partnership area and one in Gweedore.

2.3.3 Childminders (Family based childcare)

Childminders provide day care for pre-school children and before, after and holiday care for school aged children in the childminder's home or in the child's home. They usually offer the service all year round. There is, however, a huge degree of variation in the service that childminders offer, for example, whether it is full day care, part day care or flexible hours. Although the Child Care (Pre-school Services) Regulations, 1996, permit a single-handed childminder to care for up to six children, typically a childminder is a mother caring for fewer than six children of mixed ages, including her own.

There are no figures available on the numbers of childminders in Ireland - however the ESRI Survey of Childcare

---

[2] The survey was posted to 400 childcare providers. Overall, the response rate was 20% with 77 questionnaires proving to be suitable for analysis.

Table 2.2 Proportion of Children in Paid Childcare* by Employment Status of Mother

Employment Status of Mother	Proportion of children age 0-4 years in paid childcare (%)	Proportion of children aged 5-9 years in paid childcare (%)	Proportion of all children in paid childcare (%)
Home Duties	20	9	16
Full-Time Job	73	45	58
Part-time Job	53	26	39
Unemployed/Other	25	1	12
All	38	18	27

Source: Derived from ESRI Survey
*Survey did not distinguish between pre-school and full day care.

Arrangements indicate that 19% of children in Ireland aged 0 to 4 years are minded by a paid childminder and 10% of 5 to 9 year olds. Based on census figures of the population and the assumption that each childminder cares for two children on average, it is estimated that there are 37,900 paid childminders providing a childminding service in Ireland at present. These estimates include childminders minding in the child's home.

Au pairs
Some families use aupairs to provide a childcare service. Au pair placements usually involve the provision of a bed, board and a certain amount of pocket money in exchange for domestic duties which may, or may not, include childminding. It is generally an informal agreement between an au pair and the family requiring the service. The placement is associated with the attendance of the au pair at a language course. The arrangement is usually for a period of approximately 1 year. The Council of Europe drafted a European Agreement in 1979 on Au Pair placements. Ireland is among a number of countries who have not ratified this agreement.

2.3.4 Early Start Pre-School Programme
The Early Start Programme, which was introduced by the Minister for Education and Science in 1994, is a one-year pre-primary school programme for children from age 3 years in disadvantaged communities. In 1998, the programme was in place in 40 primary schools and catered for a maximum of 1,680 children. The Early Start Programme was the subject of an evaluation by the Department of Education and Science which was carried out by the Education Research Centre, Drumcondra, Dublin. Although complete, this has not been made publicly available.

2.3.5 Traveller Pre-schools
Traveller pre-schools have been in operation since 1984 and are directly funded by grant-aid from the Department of Education and Science. Between 1994 and 1998, the number of Traveller pre-schools increased from 18 to 56.

2.3.6 Provision of childcare by employers
There are a number of workplace crèches operating, mainly in the Dublin area. For example, Aer Rianta, ESB, RTÉ, Telecom Eireann, Mater Hospital, Bank of Ireland, Dublin Corporation and the Civil Service all run crèches for their employees. ELAN Corporation in Athlone also provides crèche

facilities for its staff. In general, these services are part subsidised and parents contribute to the cost of the service.

A recent initiative under the Department of Justice, Equality and Law Reform's Equal Opportunities Childcare Programme aims to stimulate employer interest and involvement in supporting equal opportunities childcare facilities. This is the Employer Demonstration Childcare Initiative managed by ADM and which is being developed in conjunction with IBEC and the EU over a period of 2 years. Eight demonstration projects located in a range of areas around the country and involving 21 employers are being supported with finance from the European Regional Development Fund, the Irish Exchequer and private sources.

2.3.7 After School Care

There are no figures available on the number of after school services in Ireland though anecdotal evidence suggests that it is a growing area of childcare. Provision for after school and holiday care for school aged children usually takes one of the following forms - (1) childminding (see Section 2.3.3 above), (2) after school care in crèches, (3) school based provision and (4) local community based initiatives.

Many centres and crèches offer a service whereby children are collected from school by centre staff and cared for in the crèche during the afternoon hours. School based services are either run by the school or by a school in conjunction with local community organisations and are commonly known as 'homework clubs'. Local community based initiatives may provide children with social, recreational and developmental activities outside school hours.

It should also be noted that in many instances, school starting time does not fit in with working parents' schedules. Some schools may provide a staffed assembly area for children who arrive to school before the official opening time.

The ESRI Survey of Childcare Arrangements, 1997 (see Section 2.2) revealed that between 3 and 5 p.m. just over 3% of 6 to 12 year olds were classified as still being 'At School' while 90% were being cared for by relatives - 87% in their own home, and 3% in the home of a relative. A further 2.9% are being minded in a childminder's home while the remaining 3.7% were classified as being at home with a non-relative.

The ESRI Survey also examined childcare arrangements for school going children during the school holidays. The findings indicate that, overall, mothers are primarily responsible for minding children during school holidays. This is the case whether the mother is classified as being in home duties, working part-time outside the home, or full-time outside the home.

2.3.8 Parent and Toddler Groups

Parent and Toddler Groups are informal groups which offer play opportunities for children (usually aged 0 to 3 years), and companionship for their parents. They are often linked to other forms of provision, such as playgroups, schools and clinics. In November 1998, there were 151 parent and toddler groups registered as IPPA members. This represents approximately two-thirds of the total number of parent and toddler groups. In many cases, the establishment of a parent-toddler group acts as a catalyst for the expansion of childcare services in a particular community.

2.3.9 Drop-in Centres

Drop-in centres are provided in shopping centres, leisure centres or similar establishments. The service is provided as part of a customer/client service and children are left for a short period of time while the parent is availing of a service or attending an event.

Table 2.3 Usage of Childcare by Mother's Employment Status (%)

Type of paid child care used in reference week	Mother's Economic Status				
	Home duties	Full-time job	Part-time job	Unemployed/ other	All
Mothers with youngest child aged 0-4 years					
Did not use paid child care	82	22	47	75	62
Crèche/nursery/ kindergarten/other pre-school	16* 17**	14* 24**	21* 29**	25 -	17* 21**
Minder in minder's home	1.0	45	18	-	14
Minder in child's home	-	11	9	-	4
Paid relative	-	8	5	-	3
Column total (Row per cent) N	100 (57) 376	100 (23) 155	100 (16) 106	100 (4) 26	100 (100) 663
Mothers with youngest child aged 5-9 years					
Did not use paid child care	99	68	84	94	91
Crèche/nursery/ kindergarten/other pre-school	-	-	1	-	-
Minder in minder's home	-	10	8	-	3
Minder in child's home	1	19	3	-	5
Paid relative	-	3	4	6	1
Column total (Row per cent) N	100 (63) 309	100 (18) 89	100 (17) 82	100 (2) 13	100 (100) 495

* Used crèche, nursery, kindergarten only (used in calculation of column totals)
** Used crèche, nursery, kindergarten plus other form of childcare

Source: 1997 Survey of Child-care Arrangements (ESRI)

2.4
USAGE OF CHILDCARE SERVICES

The ESRI Survey indicates that, overall, the most widely used forms of childcare were services of a formal nature as outlined in Sections 2.3.1 and 2.3.2 above i.e. sessional services and full day care, crèches, nurseries, and pre-schools set out in table 2.3. However, a limitation of the survey is that it did not distinguish between sessional services and full day care services. Amongst the most significant findings of the ESRI survey are the following:

- **Childminding in the minder's home is the second most commonly used form of child care overall**. It is used by 14% of mothers with youngest child aged 0 to 4 years and 3% of mothers with youngest child aged 5 to 9 years.
- Childminding in the minder's home is the most commonly used childcare arrangement among women with paid jobs.
- Use of sessional services and full-day care was largely confined to households with youngest child aged 0 to 4 years. 21% of such households made use of services of this kind.
- Over half the mothers who used these forms of childcare were not in paid employment (46% in home duties, 5% unemployed or other).
- The bulk of usage of crèches, nurseries, and pre-schools was confined to the morning session.
- Whole day care (from 9.00 am - 5.00 p.m.) was the most common childminding arrangement, being used by half of the mothers who relied on this form of care. After school care (3.00 pm - 5.00 p.m.) was the next commonest, being used by 16% of mothers.
- Two other categories identified in the ESRI survey were the childminder who minded in the child's home and the paid relative. Only very small percentages utilised these forms of childcare (see Table 2.3 for data on usage of childcare, classified by mother's economic status).
- Among mothers with children aged 0 to 4 years who were in full-time jobs, 22%

made no use of paid childcare. It is likely that fathers and other unpaid relatives (e.g. grandparents) were the main source of childcare in these cases.
- Among mothers of children in the 0-4 age-group who were in part-time jobs, almost half (47%) made no use of childcare.

2.5
PRICE OF CHILDCARE SERVICES

This section presents data on the **price** of childcare services as it applies to affordability i.e. what parents have to pay, the **costs** of providing a childcare service are referred to in Section 4.2 and 3.3.2. Although there has been no comprehensive study in Ireland on the price of childcare, it has been estimated that the price of full day care in Ireland represents approximately 20% of average earnings (Ditch et al 1998). This figure is the third highest among the 15 EU Member States.

The data presented here was derived from the following sources: the ESRI Survey on Childcare Arrangements (1997)[3], the interview and postal surveys of childcare providers conducted as part of the 'Economics of Childcare in Ireland' (Goodbody, 1998), and 'Cost of Provision of Childcare Services', a study which focused on a sample of centre-based group care (ADM, 1997). The reader is cautioned that the data is based on prices to parents of both subsidised and private childcare, and both sessional and full day care. Prices may have been quoted on an hourly or weekly basis, and the above data sources took different approaches in this regard. The approach adopted in the present report was to translate hourly charges into equivalent 40 hour weekly charges for the purpose of comparison.

The results of all three surveys cited are set out in Table 2.4 . Prices to parents are presented for the first child only. Prices are in the range of £44 to £71 per week. It is of note that the data suggests that childminding in the childminder's home is

---

[3] The ESRI survey did not distinguish between crèches and daycare centres on the one hand and playgroups and kindergartens on the other.

Table 2.4 Prices Charged for Childcare (First Child) £ per Week

Childcare Service	Equivalent Weekly Price per Child (£)
Childminder in Childminder's Home (ESRI)	71
Group Care (ESRI)	56
Group Care (Study Survey)	65
Urban Community (ADM) study	44
Private (ADM) study	46

not necessarily a cheaper option. Part of the explanation for this lies in the fact that many group care facilities are community based, operate on a not-for-profit basis and may be in receipt of subsidies through the employment of Community Employment workers. While there has been no comprehensive study on the price of childminding, anecdotal evidence would suggest that reductions of up to 50% may apply to the price for a second and third child from the same family.

There is evidence from the Survey of Childcare Providers that in group care facilities charges are higher in urban areas and for babies. Discounts of about 20% are generally applied to care of a second child from the same family in group care facilities.

In concluding this section on the price of childcare it is important to note Target 10 of the Quality Targets in Services for Young Children, one of the 40 Quality Targets proposed by the European Commission Network on Childcare to be realised throughout the European Union by 2006 (see Appendix 1.7).
Target 10 states:

> Where parents pay for publicly funded services, the charges should not exceed, and may well be less than, 15% of net monthly household income. The charges should take into account per capita income, family size and other relevant

circumstances (*European Commission Network on Childcare*, 1996, p.14).

2.6
SUMMARY

- State expenditure on childcare is targeted largely at those children in need, or in disadvantaged circumstances.
- Much of State expenditure on childcare arises as a by product of other activities and does not have improvement in childcare provision as an objective.
- It is estimated that 146,000, or 17% of all children between the ages of 0 and 9 years, avail of paid childcare.
- Take-up of paid childcare varies with the employment status of the mother: only 16% of children with mothers who work full-time in the home avail of childcare, as compared to 58% of children of mothers in full-time work.
- Current childcare services include sessional provision e.g. playgroups, naíonraí, Montessori schools and full day care, e.g. nurseries, crèches, in addition to childminders, drop-in centres and after school care.
- The findings of the ESRI Survey of Childcare Arrangements indicate that the most widely used form of childcare was a formal arrangement of the kind represented by crèches, nurseries, kindergartens or other kinds of pre-schooling. Usage of this form of childcare was largely confined to households with youngest child aged 0 to 4 years.

- The paid minder who cares for the child in the minder's home is the second most commonly used form of childcare overall (used by 14% of mothers with youngest child aged 0 to 4 years and 3% of mothers with youngest child aged 5 to 9 years).
- On average, childcare prices are in the range of £44 to £71 per week for full time care.
- Ireland has amongst the highest childcare prices (as a proportion of average earnings) in the European Union. Average full day care prices in Ireland are 20 % of average earnings.

CHAPTER **3**

Regulations, Training, Qualifications & Employment

Four issues which have been highlighted in reports and initiatives in the area of childcare published in Ireland over the past 20 years are regulations, training, qualifications and employment. These issues have also been considered by the Expert Working Group on Childcare and eight recommendations have been made which are included in this chapter. All of the recommendations proposed in this chapter have been guided by the 12 Principles of the National Childcare Strategy presented in Chapter 5.

3.1
CHILD CARE (PRE-SCHOOL SERVICES) REGULATIONS, 1996
3.1.1 Background information

There has been growing acceptance of the need for legal requirements and standards to be established and monitored to ensure an adequate level of service in childcare facilities. The implementation of Child Care (Pre-School Services) Regulations in December 1996, marks the first legislative control over this area. The introduction of the Regulations, which arise from the Child Care Act, 1991 (Part VII), was broadly welcomed and marks the beginning of a process of ensuring safety and quality in the provision of childcare services for children aged 0 to 6 years.

The introduction of the Regulations, which arise from the Child Care Act, 1991 (Part VII), was broadly welcomed and marks the beginning of a process of ensuring safety and quality in the provision of childcare services for children aged 0 to 6 years.

Part VII of the Child Care Act 1991 places a statutory duty on health boards to secure the health, safety and welfare of children and to promote the development of, pre-school children attending pre-school services[1]. The Regulations require adherence to minimum standards of safety, premises, facilities and maintenance of records. The Regulations also require service providers to notify their local health board in writing of their service. Section 55 (1) of the Act places a duty on health boards to inspect pre-school services notified to them, and enables them to provide, if considered necessary, information, advice, guidance or support. In addition to carrying out inspections of pre-school services who have notified, health boards are obliged to provide an information service to the public on the availability of pre-school services in their area.

While the Regulations impact across a wide variety of childcare services for children age 0 to 6 years there are certain exemptions. The provisions of the Act do not apply to:

1. the care of one or more pre-school children undertaken by a relative of the child (or children) or the spouse of such relative,
2. a person taking care of one or more pre-school children of the same family and no other such children (other than the person's own such children) in that person's home,
3. a person taking care of not more than three pre-school children of different families (other than the person's own such children) in that person's home (Section 58, Child Care Act, 1991 Part VII).

In 1997, a Working Group, made up of representatives of the Child Care Policy Unit and the eight health boards, was established to monitor progress in implementing the Regulations. This group was incorporated as a subgroup of the Expert Working Group on Childcare. The aim of the Working Group is to promote a consistent approach to the implementation of the Regulations and to provide an opportunity for sharing information and good practice in regard to the implementation process. It is intended that a review of the operation of the Regulations will be initiated by the end of 1999 with a view to effecting any changes considered necessary at that stage.

---

[1] According to the Child Care Act, 1991, "Pre-school service means any pre-school, playgroup, day nursery, crèche, day care or other similar service which caters for pre-school children, including those grant-aided by health boards"(Section 49).

The Regulations are limited in their provisions. The following are the main areas of concern which have been identified by the Expert Working Group: (1) notification, (2) training and experience, (3) exemptions, (4) implementation process, (5) planning and (6) the effects of implementation. These and other areas have also been highlighted in three pieces of research commissioned by the Expert Working Group: *Guidelines for Minimum Standards for Registration of Child Care Facilities* (Barnardo's, 1998), *Identification of Training Needs in the Childcare Sector*, Centre for Social and Educational Research (CSER, 1998a) and *Family Day Care Provision (Childminding): An Overview* (CSER, 1998b).

3.1.2 Notification vs. Registration

The principal difference between notification and registration is that when a system of notification is in place, the onus is on the person or organisation providing the service to notify the relevant authority. Registration, on the other hand, requires the State to agree to register or licence a service as meeting the minimum standards. It also empowers the State to refuse registration and allows for annual review.

Points in favour of the current notification system are:

*   For the first time, childcare service providers have been obliged to formally notify an authority regarding their service. This has initiated a process of establishing minimum standards in childcare provision in Ireland, and as such, must be welcomed.
*   The obligation to notify has also served to raise awareness among service providers, parents and the public in general. Ensuring quality childcare provision is beginning to become a public issue rather than a private one for parents and providers alone.

The main concerns in relation to notification are:

*   The inspection process does not acknowledge or commend good practice.
*   Following notification and inspection, service providers receive a report, but do not receive confirmation of having attained the appropriate minimum standards and therefore have no "evidence" such as a certificate of registration to display to parents or prospective service users.

The points in favour of registration include:

*   A registration system would be mandatory for all categories of service providers identified in the Regulations but exempted providers[2] could also apply for voluntary registration and be included in information lists for their local area.
*   A registration system would enable a Quality Rating System to be operated which could motivate providers to attain and surpass minimum standards thus enhancing the quality of provision within the sector.
*   A registration system would allow for systems to be developed to regulate quality in practice and in services for young children.
*   A registration system which is maintained regularly would ensure that information on services is both current and accurate.
*   A system of registration would include provision for 'de-registration' or cancellation of registration, as well as an appeals procedure.
*   Registration would apply to personnel and premises.

It was strongly felt by the pre-school representatives consulted in the course of the research undertaken by Barnardo's (1998), that registration carried more 'clout' than notification, and that a system could be structured in such a way as to provide motivation for service providers to comply with and even exceed minimum requirements.

The registration system should be guided by the UN Convention on the Rights of the Child (see Section 5.1) and 'the best interest of the child'.

The current notification system was the first step in the process of regulating the

---

[2] Exempted providers/carers would include relatives.

Table 3.1 Total number of Notifications and Inspections in each Health Board as per December 1998

Health Board	Number of Notifications	Number of Inspections
Eastern Health Board	868	101
Midland Health Board	149	93
Mid-Western Health Board	282	267
North Eastern Health Board	236	51
North Western Health Board	157	34
South Eastern Health Board	326	213
Southern Health Board	426	308
Western Health Board	305	85
Total	**2,749**	**1,152**

childcare sector. The Expert Working Group considers it desirable that this system be developed and extended to a system of registration. The Group recognises that this process will involve amendment to the current legislation and is likely to take time.

RECOMMENDATION 1:

- The present system of notification should be developed and lead to an amendment of the Child Care Act 1991, which would provide for a system of registration of facilities and childcare workers.

- All those providing childcare services for one or more children, in addition to their own, including persons employed by the parent/s of the child, either in the child's home or in the childminder's home, should be required to register.

- Relatives (parents, grandparents, siblings, uncles, aunts, and step-parents) and guardians or foster parents should be exempt from the requirement to register.

- All childcare providers who offer services to children aged 0 to 12 years, as defined by the Expert Working Group on Childcare, should be obliged to register under the proposed system of registration.

3.1.3 Training and Experience

The Child Care (Pre-School Services) Regulations,1996, do not contain guidelines for levels or type of qualifications for those who work in the early years sector. The recommendations in the Regulations of "appropriate experience in caring for children" and/or "an appropriate qualification in childcare" have become understandably frustrating, both for workers currently employed in the childcare field and for employers. There is confusion as to what these terms actually mean, and what qualifications are 'appropriate'. Unregulated training for personnel has resulted in a wide variety of approaches and programmes leading in turn to considerable differences in skills, knowledge, experience and qualifications.

In addition to training, the Expert Working Group acknowledges that recognition of existing skills and experience of staff is essential. Therefore accessible in-service training should be available to current providers (see Section 3.2 for a further discussion on training).

3.1.4 Exemptions

As a result of the exemptions that are currently in place (see Section 3.1.1), the vast majority of childminders do not come under the remit of the Regulations. Of those childminders who are legally obliged to notify, it has been the experience of the health boards that only a small number have notified their local health board. This is as a result of a number of factors including fear about income tax implications, anxiety surrounding the notion of their homes being inspected and lack of information about the Regulations.

A further issue of concern for the Expert Working Group is the age of children covered by the Regulations. At present, the Regulations apply only to those caring for children under 6 years of age. Since many children between the ages of 6 and 12 years are also cared for in a variety of childcare services, the Expert Working Group recommends that the proposed Registration system cover children aged 0 to 12 years.

3.1.5 Implementation Process

When the Regulations were brought into force (January 1997), it was envisaged that it would take health boards up to 2 years to complete the first inspection of pre-school services and that inspections would be carried out annually from then on. Inspection teams may be made up of Environmental Health Officers, Public Health Nurses or a combination of both. A number of health boards are also providing support in the form of Pre-School Committee/Steering Committees at Community Care level comprising a Child Care Manager and representatives of the NGO sector. In addition there are a range of health professionals to whom the Inspection team will report and from whom they receive advice and guidance. Provider organisations such as the IPPA, the NCNA, An Comhchoiste Reamhscolaíochta Teo and the NCMAI have, through regionally based advisors, supported the development of services and the maintenance and improvement of standards.

There would appear to be great variability between the health boards in the implementation of the Regulations. The Expert Working Group is concerned about:

- the lack of uniformity between health boards
- the fact that different inspection teams can have quite different approaches
- the lack of attention that has been paid to the training of authorised officers/inspection teams, and
- the inconsistencies regarding length of time specified for making essential alterations post inspection

There is also concern that the teams may lack the practical expertise required and are not drawing from local expertise in any formal way. Table 3.1 sets out the total number of notifications and inspections which have been carried out in each of the health boards at December 1998.

Initial inspections revealed the following issues as needing further attention:

- the need for advice and guidance;
- the need for expansion of the Explanatory Guide to the Regulations;
- the need for capital funding for service provision in all areas but particularly in disadvantaged areas to upgrade premises.

Subsequently, the Working Group, which was established by the Department of Health and Children to monitor the implementation of the Regulations identified the following problematic areas:

- difficulties with space requirements
- absence of a second adult on the premises
- poor provision of adequate nutritional diet in full-day care services
- lack of adequate toy/activities in the toddler age group
- lack of awareness concerning the post-vaccination care of children
- lack of hot water facilities
- poor sterilisation available for babies bottles and for making up formula feed
- poor record keeping.

The Department of Health and Children, in consultation with health board officials, is at present preparing 'A Guide to Good Practice' with a view to promoting quality childcare in line with the standards and Regulations under the Child Care Act, 1991. The Expert Working Group considers that a national system of registration should be guided by a national set of quality standards and procedures. The Registration, Training and Qualifications subgroup of the Expert Working Group has considered models which would inform such guidelines taking account of areas such as premises, health and safety, personnel, environment, policies and programmes in services for children aged 0 to 12 years.

RECOMMENDATION 2:

The existing notification system, and the proposed system of registration should require adherence to national minimum standards, encouraging 'best practice' which will be developed in consultation and partnership with the NGO sector.

A common induction and training programme should be provided for inspection teams to ensure that there is standardisation of implementation.

In addition, it is recommended that one member of the inspection team should be trained in the area of Early Childhood Care and Education.

3.1.6 Planning

There are inconsistencies within and between local authorities in terms of criteria used for granting planning approval for childcare facilities. Specific issues that have been identified as problematic include:

- Delay in processing planning applications
- Cost of planning applications
- Inconsistencies between inspection teams and local authorities with regard to space and numbers.

(see Section 7.1.6 for recommendation regarding planning provisions).

3.1.7 Effects of Implementation

In relation to the impact of the Regulations from the service providers' point of view, a postal survey of NCNA members revealed that the main impact of the Regulations for this group appears to have been to tighten margins and encourage more rigidity and less flexibility in service provision. Providers sought to remain viable while meeting staff ratios and paying staff a reasonable wage. In a number of cases the Regulations have meant that providers have had to improve their premises, for example, more toilets and/or alterations in the kitchen. The providers surveyed may not have been representative of the formal sector as a whole. Other providers may face much greater costs in meeting the Regulations, both in terms of capital and infrastructural cost and employee costs.

Anecdotal evidence suggests that the cost of upgrading facilities in order to meet the requirements of the Regulations has resulted in some closures of both sessional and full day care services.

In the absence of comprehensive research into childminding in Ireland, the Expert Working Group can only speculate that childminders may be limiting the number of children in their care in order to remain outside the remit of the Regulations.

3.1.8 Garda clearance

It is a requirement of the Child Care Act, 1991, that all adults working in any childcare setting should have nothing in their background that could adversely affect their suitability to hold a position of trust in relation to children. One mechanism for supporting the safety of children is the implementation of a Garda clearance system. Arrangements are in place whereby the Garda Síochána provide prospective employers in the statutory sector with particulars of criminal convictions, if any, recorded against candidates for employment in posts which involve substantial access to children.

Currently, childcare employers who are not within the statutory sector cannot be provided with central Garda clearance in relation to prospective employees. Local Garda clearance is often made available to the NGO sector within the context of 'information available at that time', but this does not equate to central Garda clearance.

References are considered standard requirements of all the employing agencies, semi-state, voluntary and private sector. The Expert Working Group considers that all childcare applicants should present references and these should be thoroughly checked both verbally and in writing before employment. In addition to references and checks, there will always be a need for clear and precise job description and guidelines, good staff support and supervision. In the UK the current registration system requires that the social services department of the local authority satisfies itself that the person applying for registration as a childcare service provider is "fit" for this purpose. They are required to take account of a number of factors including the physical health and mental stability of the individual and also to check if there is a record of involvement in criminal cases in relation to the abuse of children. The Expert Working Group considers that the issue of health checks for providers and personnel should be explored in relation to the introduction of a registration system in Ireland.

RECOMMENDATION 3:

A Garda clearance procedure at central level, which communicates effectively with local levels, should be put in place to provide clearance information in respect of all personnel working in childcare in whatever capacity.

3.2
TRAINING AND QUALIFICATIONS
3.2.1 Existing Training Provision and Accreditation

As with childcare provision, childcare training in Ireland has developed on an ad hoc basis with the result that there is a bewildering diversity of training courses and qualifications currently on offer. A survey of education and training programmes in the area of childcare which was conducted on behalf of the Expert Working Group revealed the following statistics:

- There are approximately 90 courses delivered in 58 centres including Vocational Educational Colleges (VEC's), Regional Technical Colleges (RTC's), community colleges, Dublin Institute of Technology (DIT), universities, private organisations, voluntary organisations and also in FÁS Centres and FÁS approved community locations.

- There is a wide geographic spread in relation to childcare training provision although 62% of the courses are in the Dublin area.

- Fees for courses ranged from £30 for a 1 year full time course in a VEC to £2,500 for a 3 year full time course in an independent college. Participants on FÁS childcare training courses receive a grant.

- In 1997/98 up to 4,000 people were enrolled on childcare courses.

An overview of existing training provision and accreditation in the area of childcare is included in Appendix 3.1.

3.2.2 Training and Quality
The Expert Working Group believes that the better the pay, conditions, training and support of staff, the better the quality of the service. Therefore, the calibre, skills and continuing professional development of childcare workers constitute a key element of quality childcare provision.

Childcare workers must have a liking and respect for children, knowledge about child development and early childhood education and be motivated to develop their skill and knowledge. Pre-service training of staff should deepen understanding of child development in addition to widening knowledge about the range of developmentally appropriate activities for children. As with any other professional training, childcare training needs continuous updating. Staff need opportunities to keep up to date and extend or improve their methods through planning and in-service training.

Flexible training materials and methods of learning and assessment are important particularly in disadvantaged areas where participants may be second chance learners and may have poor literacy skill. Presentation of curriculum should be flexible, practical and tailored to the needs of the participants. Furthermore, in the light of the changing nature of Irish society, it is essential that all training has intercultural and equal opportunity policies built into programmes (see also Section 5.3)

Much attention in the literature has been given to the area of appropriate training for staff working with 3 to 6 year olds. Furthermore, many books and training materials bunch the needs of under sixes together. The Expert Working Group recognises that the needs of each child are unique and that children have special learning needs at different stages in their development. The diverse needs of children at different stages of development must also be reflected in all childcare training programmes (see also Section 5.2).

The Expert Working Group proposes that a comprehensive study be undertaken into the development of the Playwork[3] sector to include a study of training needs and service development for those working with 6 to 12 year olds in childcare settings. Responsibility for furthering this could be undertaken by the proposed National Childcare Management Committee.

3.2.3 Accreditation and Qualifications

The fact that training has not been an essential requirement for childcare workers in early years services has led to a situation where there are many workers with skills and knowledge in early childhood care which have been gained through experience, rather than formal training processes. Individuals have also frequently chosen one of the many courses offered by both public and private training bodies in an effort to acquire some training in this area with the result that there is now a wide variety of qualifications acquired.

Given the lack of a national common standard or benchmark against which to measure these skills and knowledge, there is no mechanism for accrediting this experience or the diverse training courses within the childcare profession or for establishing equivalencies for the purposes of employment or future training. A NOW (New Opportunities for Women) project, undertaken by the Dublin Institute of Technology (DIT) and in consultation with all the national training and accrediting agencies sought specifically to rectify the above situation. This was the DIT/NOW Childcare Project (1996-97), which was set up to look at mechanisms to establish a national standard at different levels against which training in Early Childhood Care and Education can be measured for equivalence, and to develop a system of Accreditation of Prior Learning (APL), specifically for women who have been working with young children in early childhood care and education settings.

An APL system would also be of value to childminders, who frequently have years of experience minding their own and other people's children, but no formal qualifications.

A robust training infrastructure also requires work-based assessment of skills, knowledge and competence in order to ensure an impact on the quality of service delivery. The Expert Working Group believes that investment in training and assessment

---

[3] 'Playwork' is the term used to describe what adults do to facilitate children playing. It generally refers to work in after-school programmes or holiday schemes and summer projects but can also include work in supervised playgrounds. Playwork is generally with children of primary school age (see also Section 6.2).

must also occur in ancillary areas such as monitoring/inspections, management and financial skills. The principles, processes and procedures for assessment and certification should actively facilitate access and recognition of the various forms of atypical learning, e.g. in the workplace or community, distance and autonomous learning.

For those in disadvantaged communities, well thought out progression routes and bridging mechanisms for community specific provision to mainstream provision will be vitally important to ensure inclusive training and employment (see Chapter 4).

The Expert Working Group proposes that a national framework of qualifications in childcare should be developed to establish standards for the accreditation of providers of education and training, the validation of learners and the certification of learners. The framework should be developed in consultation with the proposed National Childcare Management Committee, within the broad framework to be established by the proposed National Qualifications Authority.

Broadly speaking, two occupational roles have emerged in childcare: those of manager and childcare worker. Some of the larger settings have developed the role of advisor in addition to these. Where a childcare worker works alone, as in the case of a childminder, the roles of manager and worker are combined. The role of advisor has evolved to support the needs of individual workers. This has particular relevance in rural areas because of the dispersion of childcare services. Generally speaking, the manager has overall responsibility for the administration and running of a childcare centre but still undertakes the same jobs as the childcare worker.

The Registration, Qualifications and Training Subgroup has following research, consultation and discussion, compiled a model of an occupational profile for the childcare sector. This is included in Appendix 3.2 .

RECOMMENDATION 4:

- An occupational profile (such as the model in Appendix 3.2) and appropriate qualifications should be agreed by the proposed National Childcare Management Committee within 12 months.
- A National Framework for qualifications in childcare should be developed in consultation with the proposed National Childcare Management Committee.
- The national qualifications framework for childcare should provide progressive pathways of awards, which can be achieved through formal and informal education and training programmes or through the accreditation of prior learning.
- The future development of the childcare sector should aim to achieve the following target:

"A minimum of 60% of staff working directly with children in collective services should have a grant eligible basic training of at least three years at a post-18 level, which incorporates both the theory and practice of pedagogy and child development. All training should be modular. All staff in services (both collective and family day care) who are not trained to this level should have right of access to such training including on an in-service basis." (Target 26 of the European Commission Network on Childcare Action Programme Quality Targets in Services of Young Children, 1996)

3.3
EMPLOYMENT, STATUS AND PAY
3.3.1 Men in Childcare

Childcare is an occupation that is characterised by low status, poor working conditions and an absence of a career structure. Childcare is traditionally viewed as "women's work" and is generally not well paid or well regarded. Poor wages, employment conditions and low status have also been identified as barriers to men's employment in childcare services.

The European Commission Network on Childcare, 1990, highlighted the fact that the factors restricting men's access to work in the childcare field are mainly those that discourage the involvement of fathers in childcare, such as cultural stereotypes and the lack of public policies facilitating men's access to this type of work. Analysis conducted by McKeown, Ferguson, Rooney (1998) on behalf of the Commission on the Family also drew attention to the virtual absence of men from childcare work. In citing reasons for this, in addition to those identified by the European Commission Network above, the authors

Childcare is traditionally viewed as "women's work" as is generally not well paid or well regarded

suspect that many men have become alienated from childcare because the wholly justified reporting of child abuse cases involving men has created a more generalised perception that all men are dangerous in the context of childcare. (McKeown et al, 1998 p.433).

Mc Keown et al believe that the gender imbalance in childcare is likely to have long-term consequences in terms of perpetuating, in the minds of children, the image that women, but not men, are the "natural" carers of children. As a result, the gender imbalance in the delivery of childcare may itself undermine the objective which it is trying to promote, namely, reducing the gender division of labour between home and work.

RECOMMENDATION 5:

The Expert Working Group considers it desirable that children should have contact with both men and women in childcare services and that the childcare sector should aim to achieve the following target: *"Twenty per cent of staff employed in child-care in collective services should be men"* (Target 29 of the European Commission's Network on Childcare action programme-Quality Targets in Services for Young Children, 1996). Measures for achieving this should be examined by the National Childcare Management Committee.

The Expert Working Group also considers that ethnic and cultural diversity should be reflected within the staff that work in childcare services.

RECOMMENDATION 6:

Employment procedures should be guided by the following target: *"Services should adopt employment procedures which emphasise the importance of recruiting employees who reflect the ethnic diversity of the local community "*(Target 36 of the European Commission Network on Childcare action programme-Quality Targets in Services for Young Children, 1996).

3.3.2 Rates of Pay

The low occupational status accorded to childcare also has implications for quality of provision. Good working conditions and continuity of care are essential for a quality service.

Continuity and responsiveness of staff and their consistent relationship with the same group of children is more easily achieved when the staff themselves are paid above minimum wages, are trained and enjoy decent working conditions. (European Commission Childcare Network on Childcare, 1996, p.23).

Table 3.2 Gross Rates of Pay in the Public/Voluntary Childcare Sector

	Junior Staff	Senior Staff
FÁS Job Initiative (35 hr.week)	£6370 to £10,010 (£3.50 per hour)	N/A
FÁS Community Employ. (20 hr. week)	£4628 (£4.60 per hour)	N/A
EHB (20 - 30 hr.week)	(Day Nursery Teacher) £9988 - £13373	(Day Nursery Manager) £12,432 - £18, 862
Early Start (20 - 30 hr. week)	(Child Care Assistant) £11,437 - £13,607	
Equal Opportunities Childcare Initiative (ADM) (35 - 40 hr. week)	(Childcare Worker) £11, 000 to £14, 000 (average)	(Manager/Co-ordinator) £16,000 - £22, 000 (average)

According to the information available to the Expert Working Group there is a wide range in rates of pay in the childcare sector. The rates of pay appear to be reasonably well developed in the public sector and voluntary sector where there is public funding for projects. This would be particularly so where there is a wage determining/bargaining structure in place. Table 3.2 presents examples of rates in the public/voluntary childcare sector.

The survey of NCNA members (see Section 2.3.2) revealed that junior staff costs average £130 to £140 per week (averaging £3.15 per hour for a 40 hour week) and senior staff costs average £160 to £200 (averaging £4 to £5 per hour for a 40 hour week). Pay rates are higher in Dublin reflecting higher prices charged. The survey also revealed that in most cases there was a desire to pay staff more, but this could not be done at existing prices.

Childcare workers in playgroups are generally paid between £4 and £6 per hour. Owners/managers may earn a little more, after all expenses are paid, depending on the location of their service, and whether they are prepared to offer extra hours, such as after school care. Pay and conditions for staff working in High/Scope[4] settings is slightly better. Junior staff in these settings are paid between £4.45 and £5.01 per hour while senior staff earn £5.62 to £6.32 per hour. However, planning, preparation and cleaning up time is paid and unlike most sessional services, where the summer months and sometimes other holiday time is not paid, staff in High/Scope settings are paid over 12 months.

Childminding, which largely operates within the informal economy, is of particular concern to the Expert Working Group. Childminding is a private arrangement between parent and childminder. Pay for childminding has traditionally been at the cheaper end of provision in Ireland. Average pay, according to the National Childminding Association of Ireland (NCMAI), is £50 a week per child, which works out at about £1.45 to £1.50 an hour. The findings of the ESRI Survey 1997 indicate an average weekly rate of £71 per child, based on a 40 hour week.

By law, anyone providing a service to children and their families, including a self-employed childminder who minds children in the childminder's home, is obliged to register with the Revenue Commissioners,

---

[4] The High/Scope pre-school curriculum originated in the United States in 1960's. Originally known as the Perry Pre-school Project, it was one of the first intervention projects established (see also Section 6.2).

and thus may be assessed for tax purposes. The self-employed childminder is entitled to deduct from gross income legitimate expenses such as light, heat, food etc. to arrive at a profit income. Where the profit income is less that £2,500 the self-employed childminder will not be eligible to become a self-employed PRSI contributor for Social Insurance purposes. Where children are cared for in their own home, a childminder will generally be regarded as an employee of the parent(s).

RECOMMENDATION 7:

A national pay scale should be established to reflect the social and economic value of the work undertaken by childcare workers. The mechanism proposed is a Joint Labour Committee (JLC) which will be required to set a JLC rate for the industry.

3.3.3 Recruitment of Childcare Workers

Three quarters of centres surveyed in the Goodbody's NCNA survey indicated that they had difficulties in recruiting or retaining staff. The major reasons were the lack of qualified people applying and alternative job opportunities with better wage rates becoming more widely available, particularly in the major urban areas. A view was expressed that childcare workers must live at home with their parents as their wages will not support them living in rented accommodation resulting in reduced mobility in the sector (Goodbody, 1998). The NCNA strongly believes that unless the value of childcare work is raised and professionalised, existing problems with the sector will deepen. The NCMAI has also highlighted the shortage of childminders.

difficulties in recruiting or retaining staff

This association is contacted by about 20 working parents each week seeking a childminder and they cannot meet the demand.

3.3.4 Role of Community Employment in Childcare

In 1997, there were over 300 Community Employment (CE) projects providing a childcare service throughout the country with more than 1400 CE staff engaged in childcare. Many community based childcare services depend on the support of CE projects to supply staff, as a source of income to meet running costs, and to meet recommended adult/child ratios.

The evaluation of the Pilot Childcare Initiative (1994-1995) identifies the heavy reliance of projects in the Partnership areas on Community Employment as a symptom of the lack of proper core funding to meet the running costs of these projects. The limitation of such an arrangement is that the funding and the corresponding number of staff cannot be guaranteed from year to year. Furthermore, the Community Employment Programme does not guarantee progression for participants, via appropriate certified training, to mainstream childcare employment, either full-time or part-time.

Similar concerns were expressed when staff and parents were interviewed as part of the "Consultation with Children", one of the research studies commissioned by the Expert Working Group. Respondents highlighted the fact that workers under 35 years are eligible for one year's participation in the programme, while those over 35 years are eligible for three years. The current practice of workers finishing on a Friday evening and new workers starting on the following Monday presented many problems with lack of continuity for staff, children, and parents involved (Fingleton, 1998).

A survey of CE projects directly involved in childcare undertaken by FÁS (1997) indicated that a small number of CE workers had received training in childcare prior to involvement with the CE but most had not received any childcare training. Six of the 53 supervisors had not received formal training. Of the CE programmes surveyed, 33% providing a childcare facility supported formal training in childcare. It is acknowledged in the FÁS report that training in childcare, though encouraged, is quite basic. In the majority of projects, CE workers do not have either enough funds from their training allowance or time to advance to higher levels of training (FÁS, 1997). FÁS are currently evaluating the Community Employment Programme as it applies to the childcare sector.

RECOMMENDATION 8:

- FÁS should prioritise its Community Employment resources towards providing a dedicated childcare training and work experience initiative.
- FÁS should continue to develop childcare training initiatives within Community Employment in consultation with the National Childcare Management Committee.
- The proposed National Childcare Management Committee should explore and support the development of other routes for those who wish to work in the childcare sector.

3.4
SUMMARY AND RECOMMENDATIONS

- While the introduction of the Regulations, which arise from the Child Care Act, 1991 (Part VII) was broadly welcomed, it is generally acknowledged that the Regulations are quite limited in their provisions.
- The Expert Working Group has identified the following main areas of concern in relation to the Regulations:(1) notification, (2) training and experience, (3) exemptions, (4) implementation process, (5) planning and (6) the effects of implementation.

- The Expert Working Group considers that a system of registration carries more weight than notification, and that a notification system could be structured in such a way as to provide motivation for service providers to comply with and even exceed minimum requirements.
- The calibre, skills and continuing professional development of childcare workers constitutes a key element of quality childcare provision.
- Unregulated training for personnel has resulted in a wide variety of approaches and programmes leading in turn to considerable differences in skills, knowledge, experience and qualifications.
- A national framework of qualifications in childcare should be developed to establish standards for accreditation of providers of education and training, the validation of learners and the certification of learners.
- Childcare staff need opportunities to keep up to date and extend or improve their methods through discussion, planning and in-service training.
- Flexible training materials and methods of learning and assessment are important particularly in disadvantaged areas, where participants may be second chance learners and may have poor literacy skills.
- The diverse needs of children at different stages of development must be reflected in all childcare training programmes.
- There is a wide range of rates of pay in the childcare sector.
- Poor wages, employment conditions and low status are barriers to men's employment in childcare services; perceptions about child abuse have also been mentioned in this context.
- Many community based childcare services, depend on the support of Community Employment (C.E.) Programmes to supply staff, as a source of income, to meet running costs and to meet recommended adult/child ratios.

CHAPTER 4

*Childcare Provision in Urban
Disadvantaged & Rural Areas*

The Government's National Anti-Poverty Strategy (NAPS), which was launched in 1997, identified childcare provision as one measure to address poverty and social exclusion. Childcare can help to combat poverty in four main ways:

- Through combating educational disadvantage among children;
- Facilitating labour market participation among women;
- Supporting women in accessing training, education and employment within the childcare sector;
- Alleviating family stress and social isolation (see Sections 1.2 and 6.2 for further discussions on these issues).

Childcare has also been identified as a significant social economy measure. The report of the Partnership 2000 Social Economy Working Group[1] characterised the distinguishing feature of the Social Economy as "that part of the economy between the private and public sectors, which engages in economic activity in order to meet social objectives" (the Social Economy Working Group Report p.5, section 1.4).Therefore, the social economy is based on principles of social solidarity and sustainability rather than profit.

Several national bodies and agreements, including the NESF, Partnership 2000, the National Anti-Poverty Strategy and ADM, have emphasised the need for the social economy to play a more prominent role both in job creation and in the supply of services in areas such as childcare and elder care. Childcare is valuable as a mechanism in supporting and enabling social and economic development and regeneration in disadvantaged and marginalised communities.

Models of service provision in the social economy emphasise the provision of services for people in disadvantaged communities by people in those communities. Childcare provision within the framework of the social economy has the advantage of retaining children within their own environment and of being more accessible to children and parents. However, as with all areas of the social economy, it is important that these models of childcare provision are properly resourced in order to prevent the development of second rate services in disadvantaged areas.

The Expert Working Group endorses the view that, within the National Strategy for the development of childcare, the needs of children and families experiencing poverty, disadvantage or social exclusion should be prioritised and resources targeted towards them.

This chapter considers the particular childcare needs of children and families in urban disadvantaged and rural areas[2] and communities. Many of the measures identified in this chapter are dealt with in greater detail elsewhere in the Report but are highlighted in this chapter because of their particular relevance to urban disadvantaged and rural areas.

4.1 THE URBAN DISADVANTAGED CONTEXT

Areas and communities of urban disadvantage are characterised by deprivation, high levels of educational disadvantage, unemployment and environmental desolation. The difficulties of urban disadvantaged communities are often compounded by increasing levels of drug abuse. There are disadvantaged areas both in the inner cities and at the outer perimeters of cities. Those at the outer perimeters tend to be poorly serviced in terms of facilities such as shopping centres, community centres, suitable play areas and childcare provision. This leads to high levels of isolation among families with young children, many of whom have been re-housed far from inner city origins and traditional extended family supports. Thus, families with children living in these areas have little respite or support in their task of childrearing.

---

[1] The purpose of the Social Economy Working Group was set up to undertake a detailed examination of the potential of the social economy, both in terms of employment and also in the supply of services, such as childcare, eldercare and services improving the quality of life in disadvantaged areas. The Social Economy Working Group was chaired by the Department of Enterprise, Trade and Employment.
[2] The Rural Subgroup of the Expert Working Group defined 'rural areas' as including rural areas and island communities.

For women experiencing poverty and exclusion, the absence of affordable childcare often means that, if work and childcare responsibilities are to be combined, part-time work is the only option. Because many of these part-time jobs are low paid, such women cannot afford childcare and have to devise their own childcare strategies. Consequently, many women may attempt to work only in the early hours of the morning, during school hours or in the evenings when older children or partners are available to provide care for children, or may have children cared for by other family members at little or no cost *(Combat Poverty, 1998)*. These restrictions necessarily inhibit their life choices and make accessing training and education difficult.

In many urban disadvantaged communities often the only formal childcare available is that which is provided by health boards and voluntary organisations, which is usually targeted at children at risk, and thus both hard to access and potentially stigmatising. Community based provision struggles for survival, while private facilities are sporadic and inconsistent in supply. The development of childcare is not only hindered by the lack of financial resources, but also by the lack of a childcare infrastructure and support systems to secure and sustain the development and provision of appropriate childcare responses.

The Expert Working Group acknowledges and recognises the Government's investment in this area, particularly through initiatives such as the Equal Opportunities Childcare Programme and the Early Start Pre-school Programme (see Sections 1.3 and 2.1 respectively).

4.2
BARRIERS TO RESOURCING AND SUSTAINING CHILDCARE IN URBAN DISADVANTAGED AREAS.

In disadvantaged urban communities and areas experiencing social exclusion there are many barriers which impact on the capacity of communities to respond to their childcare needs and demands. Some of these barriers are of general application and have been identified in earlier chapters of this Report but their effects are particularly acute in such areas. The following have been identified by the Expert Working Group:

- Due to the lack of coherence and adequate funding, many services and organisations in urban disadvantaged areas are under-funded and under-resourced. Those resources which are available are thinly spread and thus less effective.
- Access to childcare is difficult for families living on low incomes and/or experiencing poverty and disadvantage, because they lack the financial capacity to pay for quality childcare at the market rate.[3] Quality childcare is essential and requires substantial investment (see Sections 5.5 and 6.1 for discussion on quality). It has implications for cost in terms of high staff/child ratios, trained and experienced staff, safe, healthy and hygienic premises, adequate training and facilities.
- The burden of compliance with the Child Care (Pre-School Services) Regulations, 1996 on disadvantaged communities is prohibitive (see Section 3.1.1 for further material on these Regulations).
- Staff costs account for between 80 - 85% of running costs of most centre-based childcare facilities. The quality of childcare in disadvantaged communities is greatly hampered by the inability of community facilities to employ trained staff.
- The lack of an agreed progression route of training and a system for accrediting prior learning greatly hinders the possibility for women in disadvantaged communities to upskill and find employment (see Section 3.3.2). The Expert Working Group acknowledges that the provision of flexible training possibilities by organisations such as

---

[3] The cost of services varies with the type of service provided and the age cohort of the children involved. Generally, the highest cost of service provision is for children under 3 years (see Section 2.5).

FÁS is attempting to make training in childcare more accessible to women in disadvantaged areas.

- The absence of consistent and ongoing funding to resource the operational costs of childcare services has led to the evolution of a community based childcare sector which is predominantly managed and delivered by unqualified staff employed under labour market schemes such as Community Employment (CE) (see also Section 3.3.4). The majority of CE participants are not trained in childcare and are not provided with access to quality certified training once on the scheme.
- Access to childcare services in disadvantaged areas is also restricted by the absence of a range of suitable services, restrictive opening hours, location, lack of information about services and inability to access information available.
- The poor capacity of childcare services in disadvantaged areas also results in their inability to meet the particular needs of children/families with disabilities, ethnic minority groups and Travellers.

4.3
THE RURAL CONTEXT

The role of women within the rural economy has traditionally been of significance to Irish rural communities. However, the decline of agriculture output has forced rural women to seek alternative employment.

Environmental changes, including the mechanisation of agricultural work and an increase in the use of chemicals in agriculture, have reduced the opportunities for children in rural areas to play safely and without supervision.

Economic restructuring has contributed to considerable decline in population in many rural areas and to a redistribution of population away from open country into small villages and towns. In general, there is a low level of rural childcare service provision and less choice available than in urban areas.

This means that rural services are less able to meet the needs of particular groups such as women, lone parents, the unemployed, children with disabilities and special needs. The Expert Working Group considers that quality childcare services can provide enhanced social and educational opportunities for children in rural areas.

4.4
OBSTACLES AND BARRIERS TO RURAL CHILDCARE PROVISION

Rural childcare service provision is also hampered by the following:

- Low densities and scattered population increase the cost of providing services in many areas. Due to the spatial dispersion of rural areas some families and their children lead lonely and isolated lives, with few opportunities for meeting friends and playing with other children of a similar age.
- Distance and transport problems contribute to the difficulties in providing services, restricting access and diminishing the effectiveness of the service. Access to childcare services is further compounded by disability.
- The size of the workforce in small to medium businesses mitigates against viable work-place crèches.
- The development of services is made more difficult by the existing structure of services in rural areas which is usually fragmented, involving the separate provision of education, care and play.
- Lack of access to buildings within the community which could be adapted to childcare facilities also presents a barrier.
- The small size of some rural services can mean higher staff costs. There can also be problems in finding appropriately qualified staff because of, among other factors, the shortage of training programmes adapted to the needs of rural communities.
- Smaller size and dispersed service provision makes it more difficult to effectively support and monitor the quality of service provision.

- It is difficult to maintain rural issues on the national agenda, as much policy appears to be driven by a focus on urban environments.
- Rural women frequently have to meet higher transport costs then their urban counterparts.
- The remoteness of rural areas and the lack of childcare services inhibit parents from undertaking training, education, returning to work or seeking employment or becoming involved in voluntary community work.
- A great deal of work in developing community childcare facilities to date has been carried out by volunteers from local communities. Voluntary work in community childcare services is now being threatened by the increasing role of women in the formal enterprise sector.
- Policies which encourage children to be cared for in bigger towns can contribute to the shrinkage of rural communities.

4.5
BARRIERS TO HOME BASED CHILDCARE SERVICES (CHILDMINDING)

The Expert Working Group has identified elsewhere the complex range of issues which affects the resourcing and sustaining of the development and provision of home based childcare (i.e. childminding). These issues which are compounded in urban disadvantaged and rural areas, include:

- Low status and recognition of childminding as a job/service.
- Low rates of pay (see Section 3.3.2).
- The fact that childminding takes place almost exclusively in the informal sector, which reinforces its low status and pay.
- Fears about operating in the formal economy and lack of information on what is involved.
- The exclusion of most childminders from the Child Care (Pre-School Services) Regulations, 1996, which creates difficulties in terms of recognition for and improving quality standards and practice.

- Absence of local network development and support mechanisms.

4.6
FUTURE DEVELOPMENT OF CHILDCARE IN URBAN DISADVANTAGED AND RURAL AREAS

Urban disadvantaged and rural areas require childcare strategies and policies which recognise the diverse range of functions and obstacles which childcare services must address in these environments. **Childcare services must be provided within the context of local community development, targeting in particular those groups most in need of childcare support.** A key issue, in this context, is the crucial role and importance of community development and capacity building measures in enabling and supporting local communities to identify and implement action plans to address their particular childcare needs.

Therefore, childcare services should be:

- within the local community and within easy reach of the population they seek to serve
- flexible
- able to adapt to the needs of the community
- multi-functional in order to provide for a variety of needs of children and families
- staffed by well-trained workers who have appropriate pay and conditions.

Specific targeted measures and supports are required which include:

- Information strategies to support take-up of proposed schemes by users and providers in areas and communities of disadvantage (see Section 8.2).
- Specific access and support measures in relation to training which meet the needs of those experiencing poverty and social exclusion. These would include responsive and flexible design, content and delivery of training (see Section 3. 2. 3).

- In recognition of the impact of the implementation of the Child Care (Pre-School Services) Regulations, 1996, a mechanism to support structural upgrading needs to be put in place (see Section 7.1).
- Specific supports to enable the community and voluntary sector in areas of disadvantage to successfully participate as equal partners on Local Childcare Committees (see Section 8.1).

With regard to **childminding**, the Expert Working Group proposes that a strategy be put in place which harnesses the supply of such childcare services into a formally recognised sector with appropriate rates of pay and working conditions and quality standards which do not further marginalise childminding, particularly in disadvantaged communities where services are provided at low rates of pay (see Section 7. 1).

Whilst it is acknowledged that **C.E. Schemes** provide employment for disadvantaged women, they do not provide long-term employment opportunities, due to the inability of many community groups to offer jobs to workers at the going rate at the end of such Schemes. However, it is also recognised that community based childcare provision provides an important opportunity for children to be cared for in an environment reflective of their own. In addition, it provides an opportunity for members of their own community to act as providers and hence role models for the children in their care. The Expert Working Group proposes a revision of the CE scheme as it applies to childcare which will involve FÁS reallocating some existing resources under the CE programme towards providing a dedicated childcare training and work experience initiative (see also Section 3.3.4).

In order to achieve quality provision based on local needs, the Expert Working Group believes that it is necessary to offer a package of supports targeting both supply and demand. **In the allocation of funds for the provision of facilities on the supply side, specific priority needs to be given to**

disadvantaged areas. Support for the development of childcare in such areas must come from a variety of sources, including for example: small and medium sized businesses, the education systems at both primary and secondary level, health boards, local authorities, childcare organisations, and farming groups and associations (where applicable). The provision of childcare services should be part of integrated packages and programmes of urban and rural development policy, incorporating issues relating to education, training and employment and transport facilities. The particular measures and supports identified in the preceding paragraphs are outlined in greater detail in Chapters 3, 7 and 8.

Recommendation 9:

Within the National Childcare Strategy the needs of children and families experiencing poverty, disadvantage or social exclusion should be prioritised and resources targeted accordingly.

4.7
MODELS OF URBAN AND RURAL CHILDCARE PROVISION

No single model of childcare provision can be recommended for either urban or rural areas. **Equality of access and participation in childcare requires a wide ranging, creative and flexible approach to the development of services, which must be based on local needs led planning.** The following section outlines examples of five models of childcare provision which have proven their value elsewhere and which could be considered in a National Childcare Strategy. These models have particular relevance to urban disadvantaged and rural areas but could also apply elsewhere.

- Childminder Networks
- Multi-functional Centres
- Mobile Play Service
- After School and Holiday Services
- Farm Based Centres

Note: This list is not exhaustive. There are

other models of childcare provision which could be developed in response to a particular community's needs.

4.7.1 Childminder Networks

Childminder networks are a flexible and practical solution to the childcare needs in both urban and rural areas, especially in areas of scattered population. A network provides a support service for childminders and an information service for parents and employers covering a large geographical area. The network is operated by a co-ordinator who is responsible for up to 20 childminders.

Childminders benefit from the support and training offered as well as opportunities to access toy and equipment loan schemes. The quality of care is monitored by the co-ordinator. Networks can link into other childcare services in the area.

Childminder networks provides a focal point of local co-ordination and can also act as a matching agency between parents and childminders (CSER, 1998b).

4.7.2 Multi-functional Centres

Multi-functional centres usually provide a range of services under the one roof such as childcare services, family support services, sport and recreation, culture, information and adult training opportunities. The concentration of services into one centre strengthens options for fund-raising and strengthens sustainability. It also encourages greater integration of early education, childcare and family services ensuring that the relevant agencies are accessible to families.

developed in response to a particular community's needs

In outlining strategies for best practice and delivery, the authors of CSER research on childminding propose that childminders should be strategically linked to centre-based care in their local area. This would ensure a continuity of care and provide a greater choice for parents in terms of potential use of combined centre-based and family day care services (CSER, 1998b).

4.7.3 Mobile Play Service

A play bus/van can provide play opportunities where none exist and can enable parents and childminders to meet together and socialise. It can also act as a stimulus for the creation of new local schemes which could in time become self-sufficient. Equally, it can respond to short-term needs where permanent provision is not required or feasible. Examples include the Barnardo's and IPPA mobile services. Such services may also offer the facility of a toy library. A play bus is particularly well suited for work on Traveller sites as the young children are within their own environment. Playbuses can also be used to provide additional services such as health promotion and other campaigns.

4.7.4 After School and Holiday Services

After school and holiday services provide care and play facilities for school-age children (see also Sections 2.3.7 and 6.2). In some cases, this service can be provided in unused areas of local schools and community buildings, thereby easing running costs. The importance of this kind of recreational provision in a rural area cannot be overstated.

4.7.5 Farm Relief Services

Farm Relief Services are organisations that provide relief cover across the whole range of farming activity in situations of illness, holidays or emergencies. As such, the expertise could be used in a new Home Relief Services Organisation.

A National Home Relief Service could provide childcare in rural and farming communities where in many instances, a full-time service is not required. This type of service could also provide an essential back-up for the care of children with special needs. The service would require a promoter to co-ordinate services and provide operators.

4.7.6
The Cross Border Rural Childcare Project
The Expert Working Group believes that the Cross Border Rural Childcare Project offers valuable lessons in the development of a strategy for childare services in rural areas.

The Partnership was formed in September 1994 to promote the development of a co-ordinated strategy for quality rural childcare services in Northern Ireland and the Republic of Ireland. It was funded by the EU Interreg Programme. The Project identified as a key objective the empowerment of local partnerships to plan and develop childcare services to suit local needs.

Among the key childcare issues for the project communities were the following:

*   a demand for childminders;
*   isolation faced by many parents, particularly mothers;
*   insufficient playschool places;
*   lack of access to existing group-based care due to transport.

Recommendations for action by the participating groups focused on those which could be taken on board by local communities such as :

*   the promotion of mobile services
*   issue of after school services
*   urgent need for additional childminders
*   the development of support and training for those currently working as childminders (Cross Border Rural Childcare Project, 1998).

4.8
SUMMARY

*   Childcare is valuable as a mechanism in supporting and enabling social and economic development and regeneration in disadvantaged and marginalised communities.
*   The development of childcare in urban disadvantaged areas is hindered by the lack of financial resources and the lack of a childcare infrastructure and support systems.
*   Barriers to childcare in urban disadvantaged areas include prohibitive costs, inability of services to employ trained staff, lack of information and restrictive opening hours.
*   The lack of childcare provision in rural areas means that rural services are less able to meet the needs of particular groups such as women, lone parents, the unemployed, children with disabilities and special needs.
*   Barriers to rural childcare provision include isolation, transport problems, high staff costs and the absence of training programmes adapted to needs of rural provision.
*   There is an absence of local network development and support mechanisms for childminders.
*   Urban disadvantaged and rural areas require childcare strategies and policies which recognise the diverse range of functions and obstacles which childcare services must address in these environments.
*   Disadvantaged areas require specific targeted measures and supports which include information strategies, specific access and support measures in relation to training which meet the needs of those experiencing poverty and social exclusion and mechanisms to support structural upgrading of premises.

CHAPTER **5**

The National Childcare Strategy: Guiding Principles

This chapter presents a statement of principles agreed by the Expert Working Group which underpin the proposed National Childcare Strategy. The principles have been formulated following a lengthy consultation process involving all the members of the Expert Working Group. It is intended that the principles should guide and inform childcare policy formation and implementation in addition to underpinning the strategy itself. The principles should also guide all childcare services, whether they be family based or centre based, whatever the pattern of service delivery, and whether the services are in the public or private sector. They also provide reference points against which progress and shortfalls can be measured.

The Expert Working Group on Childcare recognises parents as the primary carers and educators of their children. Children learn from birth and parents are their first teachers. Parents should be supported in their role by a variety of different means geared to meeting the needs of both children and parents. Indeed, society should share this responsibility with parents. Any discussion on childcare must consider children within the context of their family and community and society in general. The role of childcare in society is to support a positive quality of life for both children and parents. Amongst the elements which determine quality of life in Irish society, as in most others, are access to resources which provide an adequate standard of living, a manageable stress environment, a sense of achievement, social interaction, progress and development. This is true for both adults and children.

The Expert Working Group has identified 12 principles which have been organised under the following headings (1) Needs and rights of children; (2) Equality of access and participation; (3) Diversity; (4) Partnership and (5) Quality.

5.1
NEEDS AND RIGHTS OF CHILDREN

- **The rights and needs of each child must be the first and primary consideration in the delivery of childcare.**

The Expert Working Group, while acknowledging that children, parents and community all have needs and rights in relation to childcare, believes that the primary consideration in a National Childcare Strategy is the rights and needs of children,

The basic principle underlying the rights of children is that society has an obligation to meet the fundamental needs of children and to provide assistance to aid the development of the child's personality, talents and abilities. Therefore, a right of access for every child to quality childcare in a safe and secure environment where he/she is respected and accepted, should be guaranteed regardless of the status of the child or of his/her parents.

The Expert Working Group endorses the United Nations Convention on the Rights of the Child. In considering the needs and rights of children in relation to childcare provision, the following seven articles of the Convention are particularly relevant. These seven articles reflect the key components of the guiding principles outlined in this chapter. The full text of these articles is included in Appendix 5.1.

Article 2 enshrines the principle of non-discrimination and equality for all children and requires State parties to ensure that the child is protected from all forms of discrimination.

Article 3 requires that the best interest of the child be a primary consideration in all actions concerning children, recognises rights and duties of parents and others and sets out the need for standards in services and facilities responsible for the care of children.

Article 12 upholds the rights of a child to express an opinion and to have that opinion taken into account in matters affecting the child.

Article 18 sets out the duty of the State to support parents with their child-rearing responsibilities.

Article 23 upholds the rights of the child with a physical or mental disability to effective access to care and education in order that the child will achieve the fullest possible social integration and individual development.

Article 30 upholds the rights of a child who is a member of a minority, whether it be ethnic, religious or linguistic, to enjoy his or her culture, to practise his or her religion, or to use his or her language.

Article 31 recognises the right of the child to engage in play and recreational activities appropriate to the age of the child.

- **All childcare provision should be child-centred in its ethos, policies, practices, curricula, premises, personnel/carer attitudes and environment.**

A child-centred service is one which views the child as the primary client and evaluates itself in terms of outcomes for individual children. A child-centred ethos also involves a commitment from childcare providers to examine their attitudes and beliefs about children and childhood. Child-centredness involves a holistic approach to children. It requires that individual children's emotional, social, physical, cognitive and cultural needs be addressed. All forms of childcare, therefore, should provide children with a nurturing experience that enhances their development and provides for their well being. A child-centred ethos is one which supports positive techniques of guidance and limit setting in order to encourage socially acceptable behaviour.

A child-centred ethos also requires providers to put processes in place which safeguard children's rights. Under the UN Convention, children have a right to say what they think about anything which affects them and must be listened to carefully (Article 12). Childcare providers should develop ways of listening to children's views according to the age and maturity of the child and discussing them seriously should be part of the process of developing practice. However, the Expert Working Group acknowledges that a merely intellectual interpretation of what children say must be guarded against.

- **Care and education are inextricably linked elements in a child's holistic development - this reality must be reflected in the ethos and programme of all services.**

Children are learning all the time. The Expert Working Group considers that it is neither possible nor useful to separate out the education and care elements of early childhood services. It is not possible to have quality childcare without having an influence on children's learning. All services should incorporate learning opportunities side by side with high quality care.

The Expert Working Group endorses the European Commission Network on Childcare action programme, Quality Targets in Services for Young Children (see Introduction), but in particular in this instance, Targets 16, 17, and 18, which refer to the educational element of childcare. These are as follows:

Target 16: *All collective services for young children 0 to 6 years whether in the public or private sector should have coherent values and objectives including a stated and explicit educational philosophy.*

Target 17: *The educational philosophy should be drawn up and developed by parents, staff and other interested groups.*

Target 18: *The educational philosophy should be broad and include and promote inter alia:*

- *the child's autonomy and concept of self*
- *convivial social relationships between children and adults*
- *a zest for learning*
- *linguistic and oral skills including linguistic diversity*
- *mathematical, biological, scientific, technical and environmental concepts*
- *musical expression and aesthetic skills*
- *drama, puppetry and mime*
- *muscular co-ordination and bodily control*
- *health, hygiene, food and nutrition*
- *awareness of the local community.*

- **Play is one of the essential experiences of childhood. It is central to all aspects of young children's development and learning. All childcare services therefore, should provide children with opportunities, materials, time and space (both indoor and outdoor) to play.**

Children's spontaneous play provides opportunities for exploration, experimentation and manipulation, all of which are essential for the construction of knowledge. During play a child learns to deal with feelings, to interact with others, to resolve conflicts and to gain a sense of competence. It is through play that children develop their imagination and creativity. The carer's role in facilitating play is to provide developmentally appropriate play activities, adequate space, both indoors and outdoors and sufficient time.

5.2
EQUAL OPPORTUNITIES AND EQUALITY OF ACCESS AND PARTICIPATION

- **The provision of quality, affordable and accessible childcare is recognised as a mechanism to achieve equality of opportunity in education, training and employment for men and women.**

The provision of quality, affordable and accessible childcare is also recognised as a mechanism to create a framework where both men and women irrespective of their race, colour, sex, language, religion, political or other opinion, national, ethnic or social origin, property, disability, birth or other status, can participate equally in society. The role of childcare services in enabling parents, whether at home, in employment or in training, to avail of a childcare service as part of childrearing is also acknowledged.

- **All children should have equality of access to, and participation in, quality childcare.**

All forms of childcare provision as defined in the Introduction, should be "without discrimination of any kind, irrespective of the child's or his/her parent's or legal guardian's race, colour, sex, language, religion, political or other opinion, nationality, ethnic or social origin, property, disability, birth or other status" (UN Convention 2.1). Furthermore, the diverse cultural, religious, social and ethnic values of all children, their families and their community must be recognised and incorporated in the planning, delivery and implementation of childcare policy. It is recognised that this is particularly important for the Traveller community and for children from other minority cultural groups.

Children with disabilities should have access to specialised assistance in integrated settings as a matter of right.

It is noted by the Expert Working Group that equality of access and participation in childcare requires that adult carers (parents, careworkers) and those who provide a framework, policies and resources to support their care should:

1. Take due account of the impact (both positive and negative) of their beliefs and practices on the type of care they provide and support.

2. Work in consultation with the child's carers and, where appropriate, with the child in relation to the design, delivery, review and monitoring of childcare.

3. Take extra measures including, where relevant, affirmative actions to ensure that (a) there is an appropriate range and choice of childcare provision for those children who have been discriminated against and excluded and (b) their communities are actively involved in the planning, implementation and delivery of services and, where appropriate, are employed in those services.

Furthermore, it is recognised that in the context of equality of access and participation for all families and children, the National Childcare Strategy will need to facilitate a targeted approach so that the particular needs and interests of marginalised children or children with special needs are taken into account in the policy making process and in the on-going evaluation and implementation of the policy (i.e. the policy needs to be equality proofed and poverty proofed).

It is also recognised that childcare has an important role in combating family stress and social exclusion, particularly within families experiencing poverty and disadvantage. A targeted approach will be essential to facilitate equality of access and participation in disadvantaged communities, in particular for low income families, the unemployed, lone parents and those experiencing poverty, discrimination and social exclusion.

Within rural communities, isolation, scattered populations, increased costs and transport facilities inhibit access to childcare services. Development of childcare services in rural communities will require a wide ranging, creative and flexible approach which must be based on local needs led planning.

- **It is essential that a national childcare strategy is sustainable on social, economic and cultural grounds.**

Childcare of the highest quality must be accessible to all parents irrespective of the child's or parent's circumstances. In this regard, the difficulties of providing childcare in socio-economic disadvantaged areas and communities are recognised and need to be addressed. Resources provided for the development of good systems of support for families should be regarded as an investment in the future of children and the country.

5.3
DIVERSITY

- **The provision of childcare in Ireland must acknowledge and appreciate the value of diversity in Irish society.**

The Expert Working Group recognises that there is a growing diversity of family life in Ireland. Childcare services and training must recognise the different family structures to which children can belong and provide for the needs of all families. In this regard, it is important to recognise the position of one-parent families in Ireland and ensure that children from one-parent families receive quality and accessible services. Inadequacies in general provision for all parents become more acute for lone parents and have increased negative consequences for their children.

The childcare environment must reflect a diverse intercultural and anti-discriminatory approach. There should be a wide range of appropriate equipment and images reflecting the background of all children including Travellers and children from other ethnic minority groups. Practices should reflect an approach which does not distinguish between children on the basis of gender. It should also provide an accessible and safe environment for children who could experience discrimination. In this regard, linguistic diversity should also be recognised and respected by facilitating the use of the child's language and that of the child's community in childcare.

The Expert Working Group also recognises that from an equality perspective, there is a great need to support childcare services through the medium of Irish within Gaeltacht areas and outside of them. Parents wishing to access Irish language childcare services for their children also need support. Parents who are raising children through the medium of Irish have a right of access to the highest standard of childcare through Irish language to support them in their childrearing role.

Target 14 of the European Commission's Network on Childcare Action programme-Quality Targets in Services for Young Children states:

"All services should positively assert the value of diversity and make provision both for children and adults which acknowledges and supports diversity of language, ethnicity, religion, gender and disability, and challenges stereotypes."

- **Different approaches to quality service development and provision are essential to meet the childcare needs of families with children.**

The Expert Working Group considers it important that, in co-ordinating and developing childcare services, mechanisms are put in place to maintain and facilitate the diversity of provision that already exists within the sector (see Section 2.3 for details)

The European Commission on Childcare Network notes that high quality services accessible to all children can only be achieved within a national policy framework

while at the same time supporting and improving the quality of such provision in an integrated way.

There is no single childcare service that will meet the needs of all children at different ages and stages of development, those living in different locations or in different circumstances. Children's needs are dynamic rather than static and each child's developmental needs must be provided for in any childcare service he/she receives.

Diversity of service provision will also require diversity of training. The tension between diversity and integration with respect to training must be acknowledged. It is necessary to provide training in environments that are attractive to the participants, especially those potential participants who have little or no formal education and training and have found mainstream provision inaccessible and inappropriate.

Access to and availability of information on all aspects of childcare is essential if parents are to have options and be able to make an informed choice in relation to types of childcare available and whether they wish to avail of those services for their children.

5.4 PARTNERSHIP

- **A partnership approach at national and local level is essential to ensure cohesion, co-ordination and effective collaboration at all levels: policy, planning and local implementation.**

Childcare services that are cohesive and integrated offer equal access to flexible, multi-functional and high quality services for all children and their parents. The development of good childcare services depends on the active engagement and the development of long term, co-operative and collaborative relationships between all the stakeholders involved, i.e. children, parents, service providers, the non-governmental sector (NGO), employers, unions, and the State.

Co-operation between policy makers at national level must be complemented by local mechanisms that facilitate involvement of all interested parties at the planning stages and at the point of delivery. The establishment and implementation of a comprehensive monitoring mechanism is essential to ensure that equality of access, participation and quality assurance is being achieved through the childcare framework.

The Expert Working Group considers it important that the proposed National Childcare Strategy should build upon and enhance existing successful partnerships.

5.5
QUALITY

> • **Achieving high quality childcare services is an integral part of the structure and implementation of the National Childcare Strategy.**

The European Commission Network on Childcare action programme, Quality Targets in Services for Young Children, (1996) states that "defining quality should be seen as a dynamic and continuous process, involving regular review and never reaching a final 'objective' statement" (see also Section 6.1). The Network notes that high quality services accessible to all children can only be achieved within a national policy strategy. This is so, however diverse the services and whatever the patterns of delivery, and whether the services are in the public, private or independent sector.

> • **A quality childcare service must be regarded as one which provides enhancing experiences for children and positive interactions between adults and children.**

The Expert Working Group regards a quality service as one that:

- offers both care and play based educational opportunities appropriate to individual children's age and stage of development;
- provides a high quality environment with equipment, materials, activities

and interactions appropriate to the age and stage of development of each child being catered for;
- has a high adult/child ratio;
- has carers/personnel who are trained and registered with the lead agency;
- offers children continuity of relationships with adults and other children;
- works in partnership with parents of children attending;
- listens to children and gives due consideration to their wishes;
- provides equal opportunities for all children attending;
- promotes the cultural needs of children;
- provides adequate remuneration and working conditions for carers/personnel in recognition of the importance of their role;
- provides equal opportunities for carers/personnel;
- provides carers/personnel with support and opportunities for inservice training;
- in partnership with parents, links children into other appropriate community activities and services e.g. library, school;
- positively asserts the value of diversity;
- is accessible to all.

It is acknowledged that many rural and disadvantaged communities face a range of obstacles in meeting these quality indicators. Lack of information and training in childcare can hinder constructive development of quality childcare services. This is compounded by low wages for staff and the lack of secure long-term funding which places pressure on such communities to focus on short-term provision. Responding to such obstacles will require a multi-faceted approach to their resolution.

5.6
SUMMARY

Needs and Rights of Children
- The rights and needs of each child must be the first and primary consideration in childcare.
- All childcare provision should be child-centred in its ethos, policies, practices, curricula, premises, personnel/carer attitudes and environment.
- Care and education are inextricably linked elements in a child's holistic development - this reality must be reflected in the ethos and programme of all services.
- Play is one of the essential experiences of childhood. It is central to all aspects of young children's development and learning. All childcare services therefore, should provide children with opportunities and space (both indoor and outdoor) to play.

Equal Opportunities and Equality of Access and Participation
- The provision of quality, affordable and accessible childcare is recognised as a mechanism to achieve equality of opportunity in education, training and employment for men and women.
- All children should have equality of access to, and participation in quality childcare
- It is essential that a national childcare strategy is sustainable on social, economic and cultural grounds.

Diversity
- The provision of childcare in Ireland must acknowledge and appreciate the value of diversity in Irish society.
- Different approaches to quality service development and provision are essential to meet the childcare needs of families with children.

Partnership
- A partnership approach at national and local level is essential to ensure cohesion, co-ordination and effective collaboration at all levels: policy, planning and local implementation.

Quality
- Achieving high quality childcare services is an integral part of the structure and implementation of a National Childcare Strategy.
- A quality childcare service must be regarded as one which provides enhancing experiences for children and positive interactions between adults and children.

CHAPTER 6

Rationale for a National Childcare Strategy

The provision of high quality childcare can have both social and economic benefits to society, particularly in urban and rural disadvantaged areas. Poor quality childcare services on the other hand, may be detrimental to children. The European Commission Network on Childcare in setting out quality targets in services for young children stated that "High quality services, accessible to all children can only be achieved within a national policy framework" (EU Childcare Network, 1996, p.10). As stated in earlier chapters in the Report, childcare policy in Ireland has been characterised by a lack of co-ordination and a lack of State support. This has resulted in a crisis in supply, variability in quality and a lack of systematic development. The proposed National Childcare Strategy is a comprehensive attempt to address and resolve the issues of childcare services for children aged 0 to 12 years.

The purpose of this chapter is to set out the rationale for a National Childcare Strategy in Ireland by outlining the benefits of quality childcare to children, their parents, employers and communities in general. The chapter therefore begins with a section on quality in childcare.

6. 1
QUALITY IN CHILDCARE

The need to ensure good quality childcare services and equal access for all children to quality services is central to the proposed National Childcare Strategy. (See previous chapter for discussion on quality among the guiding principles for the National Strategy). Definitions of quality are value based, reflecting beliefs about what we want, or do not want for children, parents, workers and local communities.

It is recognised there are numerous perspectives on how quality can be defined. These include:
- the child development perspective
- the government/regulatory perspective
- the social service perspective
- the parent perspective
- the child perspective
- the social policy funding perspective
- the staff perspective
- the cultural perspective.

Recent conceptualisations of quality acknowledge the multiple perspectives in the process of defining quality within childcare programmes and recognise that the interests of all stakeholders should be brought within any approach. Woodhead (1996) for example, proposes that any framework for examining quality in services for young children involves three dimensions: Stakeholders, Beneficiaries and Indicators.

Stakeholders may include programme managers, childcare workers, parents, community leaders, employers, funding agencies, politicians and children themselves.

Beneficiaries may include society, local communities, providers, parents, employers, and children.

Whether the values and perspectives of the stakeholders are being translated into practice relies on a number of indicators of quality. **Quality indicators** are commonly grouped under three broad categories which are interdependent. These are:
- *Input indicators* which refer to the concrete features of the programme. They are most easy to define and regulate. Examples include: the building and surroundings, materials, equipment and staffing.

- *Process indicators* which reflect the day to day happenings. These are more problematic to define and standardise. Examples include: style of care, experience of children, relationships between parents, caregivers and others.

- *Outcome Indicators* concern the impact of provision in terms of its effectiveness. Examples include: children's health and well-being, children's abilities, family attitudes.

The Expert Working Group considers that quality indicators need to be context-sensitive. They need to respond to the particular needs of parents and children in a community. Within the context of National Quality Guidelines, it is envisaged that quality statements and targets will be determined at a local level in a consultative process which will take into account the interests of all the stakeholders (see Section 8.1). Context specific information, such as that set out in Chapter 4 regarding disadvantaged urban and rural communities, would be crucial in informing this process.

6.2
SOCIAL BENEFITS OF CHILDCARE

How do children benefit from quality childcare? Much of the research in this area has focused on the potential effectiveness of quality early childhood education in combating later educational and social disadvantage and has primarily looked at the age range 3 to 6 years. The research can be summarised as follows:

- *The vast majority of research has shown that pre-school education leads to immediate, measurable gains in educational and social development.*
- *The most rigorous studies show that high quality early education leads to lasting cognitive and social benefits in children which persist through adolescence and adulthood.*
- *The impact of early education is found in all social groups but is strongest in children from disadvantaged backgrounds.*
- *Investment in high quality early education pays off in terms of later economic savings to society.*
- *The most important learning in pre-school concerns aspirations, task commitment, social skills and feelings of efficacy. (Sylva, 1995, p.94)*

One widely reported longitudinal study from the United States found that children who attended a carefully designed programme, known as the High/Scope

Programme, were more likely to stay on into third-level training and education, less likely to get in trouble with the law and more likely to be supporting themselves when compared to a control group who had not experienced the programme. When reviewed in terms of cost-benefit analysis, the researchers found that for every $1 invested in this type of early education programme, the State saved $7 per child by age 27 years (Schweinhart & Weikart, 1993).

Critical features which contribute to ensuring that early childhood programmes are effective include:
- good planning
- play based programmes
- realistic resourcing
- a positive informed attitude on the part of the staff and on-going research and development

The Expert Working Group recognises that children have special needs at different stages of development. Children under three need to be nurtured in a safe, supportive environment, in which they are given appropriate experiences which provide them with opportunities to learn.

The particular needs of very young children include consistency and continuity of care, stimulation and routine. Among the indicators of how best to provide for 0 to 3 year olds are the following:

- *staff must enjoy working with this age group and be able to respond positively in very physical ways;*
- *the best consistency and continuity of care comes from a genuine relationship between parents and carers - one that stimulates ongoing, in-depth discussion;*
- *it should be recognised that a child's known environment (where care is provided outside the child's home) and primary caregiver has changed. Hence, as much else as is possible needs to continue to be the same, for example sleep patterns, eating habits, comforters, in order to respond to the child as an individual (Griffin, 1997).*

These indicators apply whether the child is being cared for by a childminder or in a crèche or nursery.

There has been relatively little interest in the topic of after-school care compared with childcare for pre-school children. A review of the limited research that is available indicates that programme structure, adult:child ratio, adult training, activities available and the age mix of the children may all contribute to children's development and their satisfaction with programmes.

Although no comprehensive study of the impact of out-of-school programmes has been conducted in Ireland, local studies indicate that these have a positive effect on the social and personal development of children, improving their experience of education and maintaining children within the formal education system. Chapter 3 identifies the importance of 'Playwork' as a beneficial method of working with school aged children in after school services (see Section 3.2.2)

In addition to the benefits to children of early childhood care and education, there are also clear benefits to parents and the wider community from quality childcare. The National Forum Report for Early Childhood Education (1998) highlights the two-generational benefit of early care and education focusing both on the development of young children and the health, welfare and education of parents. The Forum Report includes a table compiled by an American-based Consultative Group on Early Childhood Care and Development, which outlines the benefits to children, adults, communities, institutions and society which result from early childhood programmes. The table is also included in this Report in Appendix 6.1.

Childcare has an important role in combating family stress and social exclusion, particularly within families experiencing poverty and disadvantage.

PAUL Partnership, Limerick, in their submission to the Expert Working Group state that:

childcare is an important social amenity that facilitates access to a range of possibilities for those in disadvantaged communities. These include: employment, training for employment and financial independence, respite for adults and developmentally stimulating environments, socialisation and a continuum of quality care for children. (PAUL Partnership, 1997)

Access to childcare allows adults in disadvantaged communities to participate fully in opportunities that enhance their social and economic advancement. In this regard, it can be considered as one component of a family support strategy, which aims to counter the negative effects of poverty and social exclusion on personal, family and community life.

Day care centres, nurseries and crèches also have an important role as an informal resource, offering information, advice and support on a daily basis, especially to first-time parents, which indirectly benefits babies and young children.

Parents and communities also benefit from childcare through the personal development gained in the process of collaborating to set up, run and maintain community services. The active involvement of parents in their child's early childhood care and education, through their contribution to community services, supports their own development and that of their communities.

6.3
ECONOMIC BENEFITS OF CHILDCARE

There are clear economic benefits from the provision of childcare. Firstly, the lack of accessible, affordable and appropriate childcare facilities prohibits many women from accessing employment and employment related opportunities. As a result, the economy is deprived of the services and expertise of a significant element of its potential labour force. Childcare is also a potential area of employment in its own right and needs to be recognised and supported to ensure that it can achieve its potential in this regard.

The economic case for a National Childcare Strategy is as follows:

- There are benefits to children through the provision of quality childcare both in terms of infrastructure, training of staff and quality of programmes. This in turn will lead to long-term economic benefits. Through this investment in human capital there will be a return to the economy from approximately 2010 onwards (see Section 6.2).

- There are benefits to the parents of these children. Parents will be enabled to return to training, to take up second chance education, to start their own enterprises or to be placed in jobs. This investment leads to increased employability. Benefits will return to the economy from the year 2000 onwards (see Chapter 1).

- There are benefits to employers. Skill and labour shortages are emerging in the economy which could be mitigated by greater female participation in the labour force. The benefits to employers is also evident in the increased adaptability of small and medium enterprises as they develop family friendly policies. The economic return for this investment is immediate (see Chapter 1).

- There are benefits to the childcare providers, by formalising and regulating the sector and improving its capacity, profitability and sustainability (see Chapters 3 and 7).

- Lastly, there are benefits in job creation. Investment in the provision of childcare creates new additional jobs and in particular contributes to the social economy in disadvantaged areas. The return on this investment is also immediate (see Section 3.3 and Chapter 4).

Support for the development of the childcare sector should therefore include the following types of measures:

- measures aimed at increasing affordability and choice for parents and simultaneously at improving the quality of available supply, thus necessitating both demand and supply side actions;
- measures specifically targeted at urban and rural disadvantaged areas which will provide infrastructural supports necessary to support and resource the development and provision of a wide range of childcare services;
- measures targeted at low income households to increase their access to quality childcare;
- measures that will support the labour force participation of women, with higher levels of support going to those on low incomes in order to ease their transition into the labour market;
- measures that are aimed at developing a strong, formalised and regulated sector that can provide quality care at affordable prices, as well as providing opportunities for the development of sustainable businesses and job opportunities.

the demand for childcare could increase by between 25 and 50% over the period to the year 2011

6.4
FUTURE DEMAND FOR CHILDCARE IN IRELAND

A National Strategy for the development of childcare must take into account the likely future demand for childcare.

The total labour force in 2011 is likely to be of the order of 1,899,000, an increase of almost 25% (374,000) over the 1997 level of 1,525,000. The female labour force is predicted to grow from 589,000 in 1997 to 807,000 in 2011, an increase of 37%, accounting for 58% of the total increase.

In 1996, there were 859,424 children aged 0-14 years. The number of children fell in the early 1990s, especially in the older age groups. It has been projected that up to 2011 there will be little overall change in the number of children compared to the levels of the mid-1990s (Goodbody, 1998).

On the basis of the increased participation of married women and mothers, it is predicted that, at a minimum, the number of children in childcare will increase by some 40,000 or 27%, despite the fact that the numbers of children will rise only slightly.

Predictions are sensitive to the level of full-time as opposed to part-time working. A halving of the ratio of part-time to full-time working mothers could increase the demand for childcare by another 14,000 to 52,000. However, the greatest sensitivity relates to the take-up rate among women on home duties. If this doubles, then demand for childcare rises by another 43,000 to 220,000 places.

This indicates that under a set of reasonable assumptions, the demand for childcare could increase by between 25 and 50% over the period to the year 2011.

6.5.
SUMMARY

- High quality services, accessible to all children, can only be achieved within a National Childcare Strategy.

- Any framework for examining quality in services for young children involves three dimensions: Stakeholders, Beneficiaries and Indicators.

- The Expert Working Group considers that quality indicators need to be context-sensitive - they need to respond to the particular needs of parents and children in a community.

- The most rigorous studies show that high quality early education leads to lasting cognitive and social benefits in children which persist through adolescence and adulthood.

- The impact of early education is found in all social groups but is strongest in children from disadvantaged backgrounds.

- Local studies of out-of-school programmes indicate that they have a positive effect on the social and personal development of children, improving their experience of education, and maintaining children within the formal education system.

- Childcare has an important role in combating family stress and social exclusion particularly within families experiencing poverty and disadvantage.

- Economic benefits of investing in quality childcare are evident at a number of levels: social benefits to children leading to gains in human capital, increased employability of parents, combating skill and labour shortages, improving the capacity, profitability and sustainability of childcare provision and job creation in the childcare sector.

- Demand for childcare is predicted to rise by 25 - 50% up to the year 2011, mainly because of increased labour force participation by women.

CHAPTER 7

Stimulating Supply & Supporting Demand

This chapter outlines six supply side measures and five demand side measures which will improve the availability and affordability of childcare in Ireland. This is a package of interconnected measures, all of which need to be implemented as a package in order to be successful and viable.

The Expert Working Group would draw attention to the concept of "receipted expenditure" which features in most of these recommendations. Measures to develop childcare must be tied to receipted expenditure in order to bring childcare out of the informal economy and facilitate its development as a legitimate business within the services sector. The Expert Working Group also stresses the need for implementation of this package of measures in a partnership between the State, employers, social partners, local communities and parents, within a child-centred approach.

The Expert Working Group does not see most of these measures as having a permanent existence, but as being necessary for a period to stimulate childcare until it becomes a sustainable sector. The Group considers that the measures should, in general be available for a seven year period, coinciding with the National Development Plan, and should taper off towards the end of the seven years.

7.1
STIMULATING SUPPLY
The Expert Working Group recommend **six supply side measures** which can be summarised as follows:
- Capital grants/reliefs for providers
- Tax allowance for childminders
- Employment encouragement grants
- Tax relief for employers investing in childcare
- Funding for local level measures
- Improving local authority planning guidelines.

These measures aim to increase the supply of high quality providers, to encourage all

providers to move into the formal sector and to improve profitability, employment and job creation opportunities within the childcare sector. Each of these measures is outlined in detail in the following sections.

7.1.1 Capital grants/reliefs for providers
In recognition of the fact that the supply of childcare places is currently limited and that the recommendations aimed at improving the quality of provision, including the existing notification system, entail the imposition of costs on providers of childcare, some State support for this sector should be provided over a specific time period.

At present, many group childcare providers are operating on, at best, a marginally profitable basis. There is a need to assist some providers to expand their operations and to assist others to reach the standards set out in the existing Regulations.

The current Regulations require that buildings used for childcare purposes be of a particular standard. As there are costs for the sector in reaching those standards, support targeted on building refurbishment is appropriate. Support for construction of new purpose built facilities will also encourage increased supply of places.

The State has taken action to support the construction and refurbishment of buildings on a number of occasions. This action has been in the form of tax incentives involving increased capital allowances and has been applied to urban renewal, resort development and, most recently, nursing homes for the construction and refurbishment of facilities. These schemes provide models for this type of relief.

Capital supports for three categories of group based providers are outlined in the following sections.

7.1.1.1 Community based services in disadvantaged areas
The Pilot Childcare Initiative, under the Department of Justice, Equality and Law Reform, provided valuable encouragement to

local communities in disadvantaged areas to develop childcare services for the benefit of both parents and children. This initiative has been replaced by the Equal Opportunities Childcare Programme (see Section 1.3). One element of the support provided is grant support for the improvement of facilities. Approximately £1 million per annum is allocated to community based childcare services in disadvantaged areas specifically for this purpose.

RECOMMENDATION 10:

- The Equal Opportunities Childcare Programme should be expanded so that the supply of quality childcare in disadvantaged areas can continue to be physically upgraded and have enhanced staffing support.
- An additional £3.5m budget should be allocated to the Programme for each of the first three years of the National Childcare Strategy.

7.1.1.2 Group Based Childcare Businesses
The enhanced capital allowances afforded nursing homes provide a model for the type of relief which could be provided to group based care businesses. The impact of extending such relief would be:

- mitigation of the costs of upgrading facilities for those already providing childcare services;
- encouragement of certain providers to enter the formal economy;
- encouragement of new entrants to the market.

The scope of such relief would extend not only to stand alone facilities but also to the adaptation of residences to provide childcare facilities. For new providers or for those expanding the number of places such relief should be contingent on an allocation of an agreed percentage of such places for babies and for parents requiring part-time care because of the contraction of such places due to the implementation of the

1996 Regulations. The cost of this measure would be dependent on take-up.

RECOMMENDATION 11:

Enhanced capital allowances should be provided to group-based childcare services/ businesses.

7.1.1.3 Small Scale Service Providers
Smaller scale private providers such as those operating sessional services and self-employed childminders may not be eligible for the capital allowances outlined in Section 7.1.1.2 above or for the Equal Opportunities Childcare Programme because of their private nature. Many of these are not meeting the standards required under the Regulations and are opting to close rather than make the investment required. Their profit margins are often too narrow to meet the costs of increased staff ratios and of the physical improvements required. The majority of these provide the service in their own home. For this reason the Expert Working Group considers that this category of provider should be able to avail of grants in order to upgrade their facilities to meet standards required by the Child Care (Pre-School Services) Regulations, 1996.

RECOMMENDATION 12:

- A new grant scheme should be established for small scale private providers and self-employed childminders not eligible for other supports, towards the capital upgrading of premises to comply with the Child Care (Pre-School Services) Regulations, 1996.
- This scheme would operate through the Department of Justice, Equality and Law Reform.
- A budget of £2 million should be allocated in 1999 in order to respond immediately to the demand.

7.1.2 Tax Allowance for Childminders

Childminders fall into two categories: those minding in their own home (self-employed) and those minding in the child's home (employees). Most childminders in the first category operate in the informal economy and, as such, do not notify the authorities and thus operate without any support or monitoring from the State. For most such childminders, earnings would be low and would not justify the costs of substantial control measures to ensure tax compliance. Such control measures could also act as a disincentive to continue or expand provision. In order to encourage their entry into the formal economy and recognising that they currently pay little or no tax on earned income, the Expert Working Group proposes that tax relief be provided to childminders in the form of a special tax allowance for childminding earnings. This measure would be subject to review after three years.

The Expert Working Group also recommends that relief should also be extended to childminders who mind children in the child's own home so as to increase the incentive for employment in this type of childminding.

To be effective, it is important that these measures are not seen by childminders as a means by which the Revenue Commissioners pursue past underpayment of tax. They would be best implemented in the context of an expansion of the scope of the Child Care (Pre-School Services) Regulations, 1996, to cover all childminders irrespective of the number of children minded.

The costs of these reliefs are not easily estimated. However, assuming that only childminders engaged as employees are currently in the tax net, that they are predominantly single and that their average income is £8,000 per annum, the tax foregone, if complete exemption were to be introduced, would amount to some £14m under 1998 figures. Enhanced personal allowances would cost less than this depending on the level at which they were introduced.

The advantages of this approach are considerable:

- It would provide a real incentive for childminders to enter the formal economy, thus facilitating monitoring and support measures.
- coupled with other provision (see Section 7.1.1 re capital allowances), it would provide an incentive for childminders to expand their scale of operation subject to statutory regulation and improve the quality of provision.
- it would encourage new entrants to the industry.
- it would encourage employees to remain within the sector.

To allow social welfare recipients to take up childminding on a similarly favourable basis, it is proposed that childminding income be disregarded when means testing for social welfare purposes. The current social welfare system provides payments to families which break down into rates for the person claiming, a qualified adult (i.e. spouse/partner) and children. Where a "qualified adult" takes up employment his or her earnings can result in the loss of all or part of a social welfare payment depending on the level of income and depending on the type of social welfare payment being claimed. This presents a barrier to a spouse/partner who wishes to take up childminding and earn an income. The Group considers that measures should be put in place to remove this barrier.

RECOMMENDATION 13:

- A special tax allowance in respect of childminding earnings should be provided.
- Childminding income should be disregarded when eligibility is being determined for social welfare and ancillary benefits, for example, medical cards.
- These measures would be subject to review after three years.

7.1.3 Employment encouragement grants

Under the Operating Agreements for County Enterprise Boards (CEB's), Boards are required to give consideration to the development of a targeted strategy to increase the number of women entrepreneurs and to encourage the provision of childcare services.

Employment grants are currently supplied by County Enterprise Boards. The Expert Working Group recommends that all County Enterprise Boards provide an employment grant for new childcare services, both private and community, in addition to existing childcare providers who are taking on extra staff to expand their service. It is recommended that an initial budget of £5m per annum be devoted to this purpose which would be ringfenced specifically for childcare. At an employment grant of £5,000 towards the cost of a full salary, it would be possible to create 1,000 new posts per annum nationally, both in the community business and private childcare sector. It should be a criteria for eligibility that staff appointed under this scheme should have at least a minimal level of training in childcare.

RECOMMENDATION 14:

- Employment grants of up to £5,000 for each additional new staff member employed in private and community childcare facilities, including social economy initiatives, to be operated through County Enterprise Boards.
- A budget of £5m per annum be devoted to this purpose which would be ringfenced specifically for childcare.

The Equal Opportunities Childcare Programme referred to in Section 7.1.1.1 above includes two further initiatives which involve employment encouragement measures. These are Employer Demonstration Childcare Initiative (see Section 2.3.6) and the Community Childcare Support Initiative. Expansion of this programme as outlined in Recommendation 10 would also act as an employment encouragement measure.

7.1.4 Tax relief for employers investing in childcare

At present, an insignificant proportion of employers provide crèches or support childcare provision for their workers. While large scale employers may be able to support such measures, small firms operating on tighter margins may find it difficult to do. In order to stimulate interest in this area, the Expert Working Group proposes that employers be allowed to write off in their tax returns expenditure incurred in relation to childcare for their employees.[1] This expenditure could take the form of provision of childcare facilities, vouchers for childcare, or direct subsidisation of childcare places for their workers. The costs of this concession would be determined by take-up.

---

[1] A similar concession has been made to employers in respect of the wages and PRSI payments to employees who take part in the Revenue Job Assist scheme, which was introduced in April 1998.

- Employers be allowed to offset in their tax returns expenditure incurred in relation to childcare for their employees.
- This expenditure could take the form of provision of childcare facilities, vouchers for childcare, or direct subsidisation of childcare places for their workers.

7.1.5 Innovative responses at local level

The Expert Working Group has identified two specific supply areas which require immediate development at local level. These are: after school care and childcare networks.

After school care

There is a growing need for local community based programmes which provide children with social, recreational and development activities outside school hours and during holiday time. This need arises because of women's increased labour force participation and because of the diminishing supply of part-time childcare places. Such provision could be provided on school premises or in community buildings.

The development of this sector also requires attention to the training needs of childcare personnel working with 6 - 12 year olds (see Section 3.2.2).

The Expert Working Group notes that the Department of Social, Community and Family Affairs has been allocated £200,000 in 1999 for the development of initiatives for the provision of out of school hours services under the Community Development and Community and Family Support Groups Scheme.

Childcare Networks

Childcare Networks provide a focal point for local co-ordination of childcare and can offer educational and training support and advice to childcare providers, including childminders at local level. Childcare Networks can also provide information to parents about childcare services in a locality.

The Expert Working Group recommends that, in 1999 and subsequent years, the Government allocate £1 million:

- to the development of after school childcare provision at local level which would include a specific training dimension, and
- to the setting up of local childcare networks which would offer educational and training support and advice to childcare providers at local level.

7.1.6 Planning provisions

Currently, there are inconsistencies both within and between local authorities in granting planning approval for childcare facilities. In many instances, temporary approval only is granted. There are also inconsistencies between the requirements of planning authorities and health board inspection teams with respect to space and numbers. The planning authorities are strategically placed to play a facilitating and regulating role in the provision of childcare facilities through their inclusion in development plans. These plans range from local to county plans, and include environmental and integrated plans.

- The Department of the Environment and Local Government in consultation with the proposed National Childcare Management Committee should set and publish national guidelines for the granting of planning approval for childcare facilities.

Continued

- As a matter of urgency, planning authorities should include in their development plans, planning control guidelines for the provision of a range of childcare facilities. These Guidelines should take account of such matters as the changing pattern of work, family structure, and the range of childcare facilities that is now necessary. The guidelines should also take account of the desirability of having such facilities located in the areas, including housing developments, close to where the users of such facilities live.

7.2
DEMAND SIDE SUPPORTS

The State already arranges for a transfer of resources to help subsidise the rearing, development and education of children. Providing assistance with childcare would be an obvious extension of that role. The dilemma is how best to give that assistance.

One option would be to increase child benefit substantially, leaving it to parents to decide how best to use the additional income, whether for childcare costs or otherwise. Child benefit has the advantage of being a universal benefit and would therefore be available to all families, irrespective of whether the mother works inside or outside the home or whether the family income is from employment or social welfare.

Enhanced child benefit would also remove disincentives to taking up employment as child benefit would not be forfeited by a return to paid employment. Enhanced child benefit payments would offer women a genuine choice.

The cost of child benefit as a means of supporting childcare for the 0 to 5 year age group and for the 0 to 12 year age group (the group under consideration by the Expert Working Group) is shown in Table 7.1.

Childcare costs in Ireland are in the region of £44 to £71 per week for one child (Table 2.4). To make a meaningful contribution to parents towards weekly childcare costs would require at least an additional £20 per week in child benefit. As shown by the calculations, the annual cost of £20 per week in child benefit for children aged 0 to 12 years is £728.6 million.

The disadvantage of child benefit as a means of subsidising childcare is that it is expensive and, as it is not targeted on childcare, is not guaranteed to increase the provision of childcare places or to improve the quality of childcare without a parallel investment in the supply side of childcare. For this reason, the Expert Working Group did not recommend the use of child benefit as the way forward towards affordable and accessible quality childcare. If cost was not a prohibitive factor, then the way forward would be increased child benefit as a demand side subsidy together with investment to improve quality and quantity of supply.

Table 7.1 Estimated Costs of Increased Child Benefit Payments

Weekly Value of Child Benefit £	Cost for Children aged 0 to 5 years £ million	Cost for Children aged 0 to 12 years* £ million
0.75	11.85	27.3
5.00	79	182.2
10.00	158	364.3
20.00	316	728.6

*Per Department of Social, Community and Family Affairs there are 302,786 children aged 0 - 5 years, 698,211 children aged 0 to 12 years and 1,035,993 children aged 0 to 19 years currently in receipt of Child Benefit.

The Expert Working Group recommends instead a comprehensive package of demand side measures which will provide the range of supports necessary to meet the needs of families at all income levels with receipted childcare costs in a targeted, effective and equitable way. These measures are:

- Childcare subsidies
- Improvements to Family Income Support (FIS)
- Increasing the income ceilings for One Parent Family Payment
- Personal tax relief
- Removal of Benefit in Kind treatment for childcare subsidies

In outlining such measures four categories of families availing of childcare are considered:
1. Parents who are unemployed or who are low earners, wishing to avail of training or education;
2. Low earning families paying little or no income tax;
3. Lone parents;
4. Families paying income tax.

The Expert Working Group recommends that a mechanism be put in place to ensure that 'double benefits' are not possible.

The recommendations for each of these groups and the rationale for the proposed approach and level of support are outlined in the following sections.

7.2.1 Parents wishing to avail of training or education (Low income families)

Childcare Subsidy
The economic benefits of investment in childcare from a child development and societal viewpoint have been acknowledged and particularly in respect of children from disadvantaged families (see Chapter 6). In view of this, the Expert Working Group proposes the subsidisation of childcare for low income families. This subsidy would not be confined to two worker families but would be available to low income families irrespective of employment status. Thus, parents could avail of the subsidy while undertaking training or self-development courses and work experience programmes. The Department of Education and Science has developed, with EU funding, a pilot scheme to support the childcare costs of participants in VTOS, Youthreach and Senior Traveller Training Programmes. The funds provided may be used to cover:

- Direct provision of crèche facilities in centres or in rented premises, including staff, equipment, refurbishment, rental, insurance and other overheads.
- Purchase of places in existing community or commercial crèches, (with priority support to the former in all cases where this is feasible). This is subject to payment of a maximum of £50 per week per child for a full day session, with pro-rata adjustments for sessions of lesser duration.
- Payment of childminders, subject to a maximum of £50 per child per week for a full session, with pro-rata adjustments for part-time sessions. This is subject to (a) notification as currently required under the Regulations, (b) presentation of invoices and (c) sample checks for tax clearance certificates.

The Expert Working Group recommends that the existing scheme be made permanent and extended to the childcare costs of all low-income parents undergoing any training or education programme provided by a State agency.

The Expert Working Group proposes that a childcare subsidy be paid also to parents on development and adult literacy and community education courses. The nature of the training would be interpreted widely and would include, for example, community based training or training facilitated in Partnership areas. The guidelines and eligibility for such courses should be developed by the National Childcare Management Committee, and the subsidy would be administered locally on the basis of receipted expenditure provided to the County Childcare Committees or their agents (see Chapter 8).

Both training subsidies would be means tested for eligibility and payable on a weekly basis whilst parents are undertaking training. Payment of these subsidies should not have a negative effect on social welfare payments.

RECOMMENDATION 18:

- A scheme to support the childcare costs of low income parents participating in all training or education programmes provided by State agencies should be put in place, on the lines of the existing pilot scheme applicable to VTOS, Youthreach and Senior Traveller Training Programmes. The subsidy would be administered by the relevant training or education authority.

- A childcare subsidy should be paid also to parents on development and adult literacy and community education courses. The guidelines and eligibility for such subsidies should be developed by the National Childcare Management Committee, and the subsidy should be administered locally on the basis of receipted expenditure provided to the Local Childcare Committees or their agents.

Supplementary Welfare Allowances
In recognition of the value of quality childcare provision, the Expert Working Group recommends that the current practice of subsidising childcare for disadvantaged children under the current Supplementary Welfare Allowance Scheme be broadened to enable parents, who cannot afford childcare, and who are undergoing training and do not qualify for any of the above subsidies, to purchase childcare places for their children.

An important feature of this childcare subsidy scheme would be that parents would be free to use the subsidy to purchase places from any regulated/notified childcare provider operating within the formal economy. This would help counter any tendency towards the automatic segregation of childcare services by socio-economic group.

RECOMMENDATION 19:

In recognition of the value of quality childcare provision, the Expert Working Group recommends that the current practice of subsidising childcare for disadvantaged children under the current Supplementary Welfare Allowance Scheme be broadened to enable parents, who cannot afford childcare, and who are undergoing training and do not qualify for any of the above subsidies, to purchase childcare places for their children.

> *the need to support those families with receipted childcare costs whose incomes are so low that they pay little or no tax*

7.2.2 Family Income Supplement (FIS) for low earning families

The Expert Working Group recognises the need to support those families with receipted childcare costs whose incomes are so low that they pay little or no tax and would, therefore, not benefit from tax relief on childcare costs. In such cases, earnings are likely to be low relative to childcare costs, so that the net return from working is small or non-existent.

At present, to be eligible for FIS, a couple with children must have a combined total of at least 38 hours work per fortnight and have earnings below specified income limits. FIS is payable at a rate of 60% of the difference between the weekly income and a specified income limit for each family size. The scheme was restructured in 1998 and is now based on income net of tax rather than gross income. At present, there are very few two earner couples benefiting from FIS. This may reflect the fact that payments under FIS are not sufficient to offset childcare costs.

The Expert Working Group recommends that the specified income limit for FIS should be raised on a case by case basis where families incur receipted childcare costs. For example, if the revised FIS scheme were to assist a two worker family with one child for childcare expenses of £30 per week, then the specified income limit would need to be raised by £50. Higher increases would be granted to families with more than one child. At this level of payment low income families would receive a greater level of support for childcare expenses than higher income families would through the tax measure outlined in Section 7.2.4.

The costs of implementing this policy are difficult to ascertain as it is dependent on take-up. It is of note that some families may be eligible to benefit both from tax relief measures and FIS supports. However, as stated earlier, 'double benefits' should not be possible.

RECOMMENDATION 20:

The specified income limit for Family Income Supplement should be raised on a case by case basis where families incur receipted childcare costs.

7.2.3 Lone Parents
One Parent Family Payment

Children in lone-parent families face a higher risk of poverty than children in two-parent families. Participation in employment, represents the best prospect for improving income and hence the living standards of lone parents and their children (Commission on the Family, 1998).

Under the current scheme for lone parents administered by the Department of Social, Community and Family Affairs, a lone parent receives £85.70 for himself/herself and a first child and an amount of £15.20 is paid in respect of each subsequent child. Earnings up to £6,000 a year do not affect entitlement to the full weekly payment, and a lone parent earning up to £12,000 can retain entitlement to some weekly payment. Figure 7.1 (Goodbody, 1998) illustrates the impact of childcare costs on net household income of lone parents with two children. It can be seen that a poverty trap exists above £12,000 of earnings when the social welfare payment is completely withdrawn. The Expert Working Group recommends that the One Parent Family Payment scheme be expanded to increase the ceiling of earnings to £16,000 on a case by case basis where parents incur receipted childcare costs.

Fig 7.1: Impact of Childcare costs on Net Household Income of Lone Parents

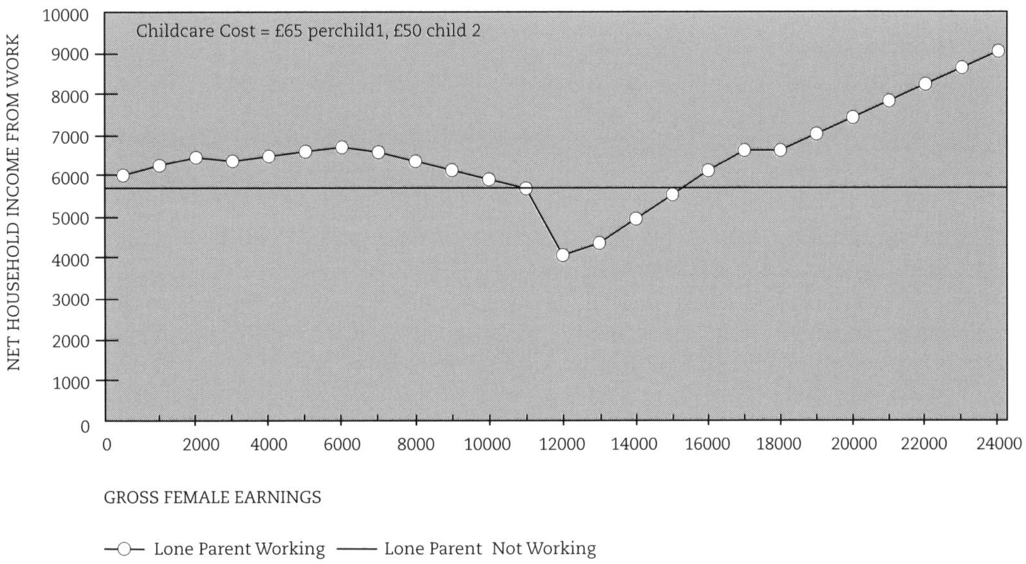

Childcare Cost = £65 perchild1, £50 child 2

Y-axis: NET HOUSEHOLD INCOME FROM WORK (0 to 10000)

X-axis: GROSS FEMALE EARNINGS (0 to 24000)

—○— Lone Parent Working ——— Lone Parent Not Working

7.2.4 Tax relief

Childcare costs are a significant barrier to the labour force participation of women whether their spouse is in employment or unemployed. Disincentives facing married women in taking up work arise because additional earnings are offset by the relatively high marginal rates of taxation and by the costs of providing childcare. The scale of the disincentive is large, implying that any tax relief measure would have to offset a significant portion of childcare costs. At 1998 prices, the annual price of full-time childcare is in excess of £3,000.

The disincentive to work applies even where the income of the household is large. This supports the view, therefore, that tax relief should be generally available to parents with different levels of family income. However, to ensure some element of equity in the relief, it should be granted at the standard tax rate only.

Because a family's childcare costs are directly related to the number of children in childcare, it is considered that the tax relief should be given in respect of each relevant child. However, the price of childcare for a second child is generally reduced by some 20%. Childcare costs are also less in respect of school children who require after school care only. It would be appropriate therefore that the level of tax relief be similarly reduced in these circumstances.

The Expert Working Group endorses the view that there should be universal implementation of tax relief, that is, it should be applicable to all family units who use childcare including those with one earner. Therefore, the Expert Working Group proposes a tax relief measure which would have the following attributes:

•   relief on receipted childcare expenses of up to £4,000 per child per annum to be granted to all family units

•   relief to be granted in respect of children aged 0 to 12 years and at the standard tax rate

- allowances to be in respect of each child, with the allowance for first child under 5 years[2] at £4,000 per annum, and subsequent children at £3,200; the allowance for children 5 years and over (school going children) to be at £2,000 per annum. The value of this allowance would be £1,040 per annum or £20 per week for the first child.

Important features of the implementation of the proposed tax relief is that it would be based on a "receipted" concept and would be granted solely in respect of childcare services purchased from providers who are registered under the proposed registration system and have met the requirements of the Child Care (Pre-School Services) Regulations, 1996, (see Section 3.1).

RECOMMENDATION 22:

A tax relief measure at the standard rate is proposed which would grant:
- relief on receipted childcare expenses of up to £4,000 per child per annum to all family units who use childcare in respect of children aged 0 to 12 years.
- allowances in respect of each child, with the allowance for first child under 5 years at £4,000 per annum, and subsequent children at £3,200.
- allowances for children 5 years and over (school going children) at £2,000 per annum.

Costs of Tax Relief

The allowance of £4,000 which is proposed is equivalent to childcare prices of £80 per week for 50 weeks in the year. The various surveys quoted in Section 2.5 estimated that the weekly price of childcare is in the range of £44 to £71 per week. Thus, some taxpayers who require full time childcare will not make use of the full allowance. However, given that childcare charges are rising, it would be judicious not to make any downward adjustment to costs to reflect this.

Under-usage of the full allowances could also arise where married two earner families require only part-time childcare. This would occur mainly where the mother is in part-time employment only. The ESRI survey indicates that 45% of married women in the workforce are working part-time. This indicates that the costs for two earner families should be factored downwards by 22.5%.

Parents who work full-time in the home are least likely to use their full allowances. These parents normally avail of playgroup or other sessional pre-school facilities only. The most typical pattern of use is for half day care or for two to three hours per day care during school terms. For costing purposes, it is assumed that there is a weekly charge of £30 for 33 weeks of the year i.e. an expenditure of almost £1,000 or one quarter of the full allowance. This means that the cost for one earner families should be factored downward by 75%.

Based on adjustments to reflect the above factors, the costs of tax relief based on 1998 figures are given in Table 7.2. The tax allowance of £4,000 for the first child and pro-rata allowances for other children would cost £30m in a full year based on existing levels of use of paid childcare arrangements (see Table 2.3).

As the relief would be given in arrears, the bulk of this cost would not arise until the end of the first year of implementation.

It should be noted that this proposal to grant tax relief in respect of childcare costs is not without precedent. Many specifically targeted allowances already exist in the tax code. These include the PAYE allowance, the allowance for employment of a carer for an incapacitated person or their incapacitated spouse and the more recent Revenue Job Assist Allowance.

Future Cost of Childcare Tax Relief

If all childcare were to be immediately receipted the costs would increase from £30m to £66m (Goodbody, 1998). However,

---

[2] For the purposes of the calculation of the costs of tax relief, the researchers were limited to the age bands of the census statistics. The Expert Working Group notes that these are not consistent with the compulsory school starting age of 6 years.

Table 7.2 Cost of tax relief on receipted childcare expenditure

Allowance Per First Child	Children under Five Years		Children over Five Years	All Children under 12 years
	First Child	Other Children		
	£m	£m	£m	£m
£1,000	4.1	3.5	2.4	9.9
£2,000	8.3	7.1	4.6	20.1
£3,000	10.1	8.6	5.5	24.0
£4,000	12.1	10.3	7.2	29.6

Note: some figures do not tally due to rounding

this would require that all childcare would take place in the formal economy.

7.2.5 Benefit in Kind treatment of subsidised childcare

If tax relief is granted to parents who are purchasing their own childcare then, on consistency grounds, free or subsidised workplace childcare should no longer be treated as benefit in kind for income taxation purposes. Similar benefit in kind/fringe benefit tax exclusions for employer funded childcare facilities have been provided in the UK and Australia.

> **RECOMMENDATION 23:**
>
> Free or subsidised workplace childcare should no longer be treated as benefit in kind for income taxation purposes.

7.2.6 Impact of the demand side supports

These demand side measures are structured to ensure that childcare costs are mitigated for parents at all levels: the childcare subsidy will benefit those in low income and unemployed households, FIS will benefit low income working households and tax relief will benefit mainly those in middle and higher income households. The structure of the reliefs offered is such that the low income households stand to benefit to the greatest extent.

The impact of these measures obviously depends on take-up. However, the evidence presented in this report suggests that there will be positive impacts on the economy through increased labour market participation, increased job creation in the sector, maintenance of human capital and ultimately through the development of children into productive adults thus giving cost benefit.

7.2.7

The 1999 Budget contains a move towards a Tax Credit system. If this trend continues into future budgets and tax allowances are replaced by tax credits, then Refundable Tax Credits could become an option and could replace the Expert Working Group's recommendations in relation to income tax, FIS and other demand side subsidies.

> **RECOMMENDATION 24:**
>
> If a tax credit system is introduced, the Expert Working Group's recommendations in relation to tax, FIS and other demand side subsidies should be replaced by Refundable Tax Credits.

CHAPTER 8

Local Planning & National Co-ordination

The Expert Working Group recommends an enhanced role for the State in a National Childcare Strategy which provides the infrastructural and policy framework to support and facilitate the development of the childcare sector in Ireland.

Chapter Seven sets out policy recommendations which outline measures which stimulate demand and supply by supporting families and childcare providers. It is essential that changes in policy at central level be complemented by strategies both at national and local level which ensure a co-ordinated and integrated approach to childcare, facilitating the development of multi-functional, accessible and quality childcare services.

Childcare provision should reflect and be responsive to the local community context and needs. Services should be integrated, addressing a range of different needs for both parents and children. The particular issues of disadvantaged communities and

groups in terms of resourcing and enabling them to identify, articulate and respond to childcare needs in their area need to be taken into account.

Therefore, the Expert Working Group recommends that the implementation of a National Childcare Strategy take place in the context of local needs-led planning, involving consultation and participative planning of all the stakeholders.

In order to facilitate this process, the Expert Working Group proposes that the following structures and mechanisms be put in place:
• County Childcare Committees;
• A National Childcare Management Committee;
• An Interdepartmental Policy Committee on Childcare.

It is proposed that the links between structures be supportive, to ensure that experiences and knowledge are shared. This is reflected in Figure 8.1 which represents the Framework, including the

Figure 8.1 National Childcare Framework: Local Planning and National Co-ordination

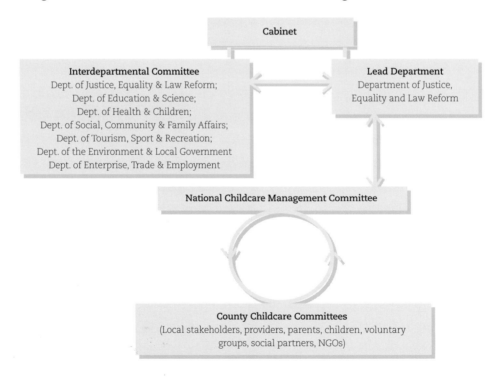

structures identified above. These structures represent a template for needs-led planning and national co-ordination that has been agreed by the Expert Working Group. On acceptance by Government, the National Childcare Management Committee will put in place operational procedures and guidelines through a consultative mechanism.

8.1
LOCAL PLANNING AND DEVELOPMENT: COUNTY CHILDCARE COMMITTEES

8.1.1 Objectives
The primary task of the County Childcare Committees would be to develop a seven year **County Childcare Plan** which would be submitted to the National Childcare Management Committee for appraisal and evaluation.

Each plan would be based on local needs-led planning, consultation and development. It would contain terms of reference, an analysis of current provision and supply, a demographic profile, an analysis of future demand and priority objectives for the area, in addition to targets and schedules.

County Childcare Plans would form an element of the 'County Development Plan' (see 7.1.6). The County Childcare Committees should, therefore, work in close co-operation with the local authorities.

Underpinning each plan would be the **Guiding Principles** of the Proposed National Childcare Strategy, which are outlined in Chapter Five and presented under five headings: needs and rights of children, equal opportunities and equality of access and participation, diversity, partnership and quality.

Following agreement on the strategy of a County Childcare Plan, it would be the work of the County Childcare Committee to monitor its implementation.
Crucial to the success of the work of the

County Childcare Committees in this regard would be the development of a local **strategy for co-ordination and development** which would build on existing successful partnerships and maximise existing resources including the adaptation of buildings in the community such as community centres for use as childcare facilities. Such a strategy would take into account county specific information, such as needs assessment, in addition to the training of personnel, on-going in-service training and support for workers.

As the achievement of high quality childcare services for all children is a central feature of the proposed National Childcare Strategy, it would be essential that each County Childcare Committee set down **quality statements and targets** which will take into account the interests of all the stakeholders.

Childcare provision needs to be accessible, appropriate and capable of catering for children with special needs and children from different cultural backgrounds. In order to ensure that equality of access and participation and quality assurance was being achieved, each County Childcare Committee would also be required to establish and implement a comprehensive **monitoring and evaluation mechanism**.

The development of an **information strategy** whereby all parents have access to information on all aspects of childcare would also be under the remit of the County Childcare Committee.

In summary: A **County Childcare Plan** should contain:
• terms of reference
• demographic profile of the area
• analysis of current provision and supply
• analysis of future demand
• priority objectives for the area
• specific special needs and social inclusion measures
• quality statements and targets
• information strategy

- strategy for co-ordination and development
- needs analysis.

8.1.2 Membership

Each County Childcare Committee would be established under agreed criteria set down centrally (i.e. National Childcare Management Committee) and would consist of representatives from all the relevant cross sector local stakeholders, i.e.:

- local providers, both private and community,
- NGO/Childcare sector,
- statutory bodies/agencies,
- social partners and other related personnel with specific expertise,
- Parents.

In total, approximately 30 County Childcare Committees would be established, one for each county, with larger counties being subdivided. County Childcare Committees would have independent status and would be legally constituted in order to employ staff directly and channel finance. The Expert Working Group proposes that the **local authorities** be charged with convening the Childcare Committees. Administrative costs would be sourced from the National Childcare Management Committee.

Each Committee would appoint a **Co-ordinator** who would oversee the development and implementation of the County Childcare Plan on behalf of the County Childcare Committee. The Co-ordinator would have the experience, capacity and understanding of the childcare sector necessary to work with the various interests involved.

8.1.3 Resourcing and Financing the County Childcare Committees

The Expert Working Group recommends that the funding of the County Childcare Plans be placed on a firm footing to ensure that County Childcare Committees are able to plan strategically in the interests of the provision of quality childcare in their area.

The Expert Working Group proposes that in relation to 1999, the Government allocate £2 million for the establishment, development and implementation of county structures.

Further resources which would be supplied to each County Childcare Committee include the following:

- Mapping Documents - resources have already been agreed and have been made available by the EU to the Department of Justice, Equality and Law Reform, to undertake a national childcare census of group settings. This will result in county reports showing clearly the services currently available.
- Central guidelines and support from the National Childcare Management Committee (see Section 8.2).

Internal resources which the County Childcare Committees would draw on include:

- the local resources in terms of documentation, studies, reports, analysis of the needs of the area;
- the expertise and experience of the direct membership of the County Childcare Committee in addition to the wider network;
- administrative support, particularly from the local authority, to service the County Childcare Committee.

Existing and increased budget lines for childcare would remain with the appropriate department/agency/voluntary organisation. However, these would now operate within an agreed county strategy.

- County Childcare Committees, consisting of representatives from all the relevant cross sector local stakeholders be established.
- The primary focus of the Committees would be the development, implementation and monitoring of a seven year County Childcare Plan.
- The County Childcare Committee should co-ordinate the new and existing services within the area and monitor implementation of the Plan against agreed targets, which should be set by all the stakeholders.
- A budget of £2million should be allocated for 1999 for the establishment, development and implementation of county structures.

8.2
NATIONAL PLANNING AND CO-ORDINATION: NATIONAL CHILDCARE MANAGEMENT COMMITTEE

The overall aim of the National Childcare Management Committee would be to support, appraise, resource and monitor the County Childcare Plans and recommend policy developments to enhance national co-ordination.

8.2.1 Objectives

The Expert Working Group proposes that specific responsibilities of the National Childcare Management Committee be the following:

- The development of **national guidelines on quality standards for provision.**
- The development of **national guidelines on the standardisation, accreditation and quality-proofing of training in childcare**
- **Monitoring the work of County Childcare Committees by:**
  - agreeing targets with County Childcare Committees

  - evaluating the County Childcare Plans and monitoring their implementation against specific indicators, and
  - the provision of information and support to the County Childcare Committees.

The Expert Working Group recommends that this should be undertaken in a spirit of partnership, whereby the National Childcare Management Committee and the Local Childcare Committee would benefit from and be informed by the expertise and experience of the other. This is reflected in Figure 8.1 which illustrates the conceptual framework of the proposed National Childcare Strategy.

- **Undertaking research** - the present Report has highlighted gaps in knowledge in relation to childcare in Ireland such as after-school care and playwork and absence of childminding data.
- The National Childcare Management Committee would also play a role in **policy development**. This would be facilitated by its formal link with the Department of Justice, Equality and Law Reform and other Government departments through the Interdepartmental Committee. The National Childcare Management Committee should also support the dissemination of models of good practice and the development of models of inclusion.

The National Childcare Management Committee would have **independent status** and be legally constituted to employ a paid executive with the appropriate childcare skills and experience to perform the necessary functions under the direction of the Management Committee.

The National Childcare Management Committee would liaise directly with the Department of Justice, Equality and Law Reform, the designated lead department for the proposed National Childcare Strategy.

The specific remit of the lead department would be to facilitate the co-ordination of the range of childcare services across departments and to strengthen and enhance the interface between all departments with a direct and indirect role in childcare. The Expert Working Group recommends that each department would maintain its budget line and continue its primary remit in this area. This will ensure a partnership approach. In this regard it is also proposed that an **Interdepartmental Policy Committee on Childcare** should be established which will operate as a link between Cabinet and the National Childcare Committee. The Committee would be consist of assistant secretaries from the relevant departments and would be chaired by the Department of Justice, Equality and Law Reform.

8.2.2 Membership

The National Childcare Management Committee should be constituted, as far as possible, to reflect the same cross sector representation as the County Childcare Committee. It would also have representation from the County Childcare Committees and specialist expertise.

8.2.3 Resourcing and financing the National Childcare Management Committee

The Expert Working Group proposes that in relation to 1999, that the Government allocate:

- £0.5 million for the establishment and research and development costs of the National Childcare Management Committee.

- £0.5 million to national/regional childcare organisations of a voluntary nature, who can demonstrate a capacity to support the implementation of the National Childcare Strategy.

The total budget required for 1999 would therefore be £6 million to begin the implementation of the seven year Childcare Strategy which is summarised in Section 8.3.

RECOMMENDATION 26:

- A National Childcare Management Committee should be established with the same cross sector representation as the County Childcare Committees.
- The key objective of the Committee would be to support, appraise, resource and monitor County Childcare Plans in addition to the co-ordination of existing national developments in the childcare field, and informing national policy development.
- A budget of £0.5 million should be allocated for 1999 for the establishment and research and development costs of the National Childcare Management Committee.
- A budget of £0.5 million should be allocated for 1999 for national/regional childcare organisations of a voluntary nature, who can demonstrate a capacity to support the implementation of the National Childcare Framework.

RECOMMENDATION 27:

- The Department of Justice, Equality and Law Reform should be the designated lead department with respect to the National Strategy for Childcare.
- This remit would be to facilitate the co-ordination of the range of childcare services across departments, to strengthen and enhance the interface between all departments with a direct and indirect role in childcare.
- An Interdepartmental Policy Committee on Childcare should be established which will operate as a link between Cabinet and the National Childcare Management Committee.
- The Interdepartmental Policy Committee should also consider the recommendations of other relevant reports, including the Report of the Commission on the Family (1998) and the Report on the National Forum for Early Childhood Education (1998).

8.3
KEY OBJECTIVES FOR 1999

In order to respond immediately to the crisis in childcare supply and demand, the Expert Working Group proposes the following key objectives for 1999 to begin the implementation of the seven year National Childcare Strategy.

- The establishment of County Childcare Committees consisting of representatives from all the relevant cross sector stakeholders. In relation to 1999, it is proposed that the Government allocate £2 million for the establishment, development and implementation of the county structures.
- The establishment of a National Childcare Management Committee with the same cross sector representation as the County Childcare Committees.
- The Expert Working Group proposes that in relation to 1999, that the Government allocate:
  - £0.5 million for the establishment and research and development costs of the National Childcare Management Committee.
  - £0.5 million to national/regional childcare organisations of a voluntary nature, who can demonstrate a capacity to support the implementation of the National Childcare Framework.
- A new grant scheme should be established for small scale private providers and self-employed childminders, not eligible for other supports, towards the capital upgrading of premises to comply with the Child Care (Pre-School Services) Regulations, 1996. A budget of £2 million should be allocated in 1999 in order to respond immediately to demand.

- After school care and childcare networks have been identified as requiring immediate development. In relation to 1999, it is proposed that £1 million be allocated to the development of after-school childcare provision and for the setting up of local childcare networks.
- The total budget required for 1999 to begin the implementation of the seven year Childcare Strategy would therefore be £6 million.

Bibliography, Appendices & Glossary

Bibliography

Abbott, L. & Moylett, H. (eds.) 1997, *Working with the under 3's: Responding to Children's Needs*. Buckingham: Open University Press.

Barnardo's National Children's Resource Centre *(1998), Research guidelines for minimum standards for registration of childcare facilities*: Unpublished draft report to the Subgroup on Registration, Training and Qualifications of the Expert Working Group on Childcare.

Barnett, W.S. (1996), *Lives in the balance: Age 27 benefit - cost analysis of the High/Scope Perry Preschool Program*, Monographs of the High/Scope Educational Research Foundation Number Eleven, Michigan: High/Scope Press.

Boldt, S. & Devine, B. (1998), Educational disadvantage in Ireland: Literature review and summary report in *Educational Disadvantage and Early School Leaving*, Dublin: The Combat Poverty Agency.

Callan, T. & Farrell, B. (1991), *Women's participation in the labour market*, Dublin: National Economic and Social Council.

Central Statistics Office (1996), *Labour Force Survey*.

Central Statistics Office (1998a), *Labour Force Survey*

Central Statistics Office (1998b), *Statistical Release, Quarterly National Household Survey, 1997. Dublin: The Stationery Office*

Centre for Social and Educational Research, DIT (1998), *Identification of training needs of the childcare sector*: Unpublished report undertaken on behalf of the subgroup on Registration, Training and Qualifications of the Expert Working Group on Childcare.

Centre for Social and Educational Research, DIT (1998), *Study of family day care (childminding) provision: an overview*. Unpublished report to the Sub-group on Resourcing and Sustaining Childcare within Urban Disadvantaged Areas.

Clarke, M. (1997), *Briefing document on childcare background information*: Prepared for the Expert Working Group on Childcare (unpublished).

Cohen, B. & Fraser, N. (1991), *Childcare in a modern welfare system: Towards a new national policy*. IPPR Social Policy Paper, No. 6. London: Institute for Public Policy Research.

Combat Poverty Agency (1998), *The role of childcare in tackling poverty*: Submission to the Expert Working Group on Childcare. Dublin: The Combat Poverty Agency.

Commission on the Family (1998), *Strengthening families for life*: Final report of the Commission on the Family to the Minister for Social, Community and Family Affairs. Dublin: The Stationery Office.

Coolahan, J. (ed.) (1998), *Report on the National Forum for Early Childhood Education,* Dublin: The Stationery Office.

Cross Border Rural Childcare Project (1998), *Needs led planning for quality early years service in rural areas*.

Department of Enterprise, Trade and Employment (1998), *Employment Action Plan: Ireland*.

Department of Enterprise, Trade and Employment (1998), *Report of the Partnership 2000 Social Economy Working Group*.

Department of Health (1996), *Child Care (Pre-School Services) Regulations, 1996*. Dublin: The Stationery Office.

Department of Labour (1994), *Report of the Working Group on Childcare Facilities for Working Parents*. Dublin: The Stationery Office.

Ditch, J., Barnes, H., Bradshaw, J. & Kilkey, M (1998), *European Observatory on National Family Studies, A synthesis of National Family*

Policies, 1996, York: University of York, Social Policy Research Unit.

Dublin Institute of Technology/NOW (1997) Final Report of DIT/NOW OMNA I project: Dublin: Dublin Institute of Technology.

Economic and Social Research Institute (1998), *Budget Perspectives - Proceedings of a Conference held on 27th October, 1998 - Childcare Policy (Ch 5) by Dr. Tony Fahey, ESRI.*

European Commission Network on Childcare (1990) *Men as carers of children,* Brussels: European Commission.
European Commission Network on Childcare (1996), *Quality Targets in Services for Young Children,* Brussels: European Commission.

Fingleton, M. (1998), *Consultation with children and parents*: Results of a consultation project carried out with children, parents and staff at four childcare locations on behalf of the Expert Working Group on Childcare (unpublished).

Goodbody Economic Consultants in association with The Economic and Social Research Institute, the Department of Psychology, University College, Dublin and The Policy Studies Institute, U.K. (1998) *The Economics of Childcare.* Unpublished report prepared on behalf of the Expert Working Group on Childcare.

Government of Ireland (1996), *Partnership 2000 for Inclusion, Employment and Competitiveness,* Dublin: The Stationery Office.

Government of Ireland (1996), *Sharing in Progress*: National Anti-Poverty Strategy, Dublin: The Stationery Office.

Griffin, B. (1992), 'The child should feel good enough' - nurturing a sense of self in young children in Abbott, L. & Moylett, H. (eds.) 1997, *Working with the under 3's: Responding to Children's Needs.* Buckingham: Open University Press.

Hayes, N. (1995), *The case for a national policy on early education,* Poverty and Policy discussion paper No. 2, Dublin: The Combat Poverty Agency.

Hayes, N. & Moore, N. (1998), *Quality in services for young children in rural areas.* Unpublished report to the Cross Border Rural Childcare Project.

Hohmann, M. and Weikart, D. (1995), *Educating Young Children:* Michigan: The High/Scope Press.

Isis Research Group, Trinity College Dublin (1998), *Caring for all our futures: Policy recommendations for establishing a national childcare strategy based on successful NOW-funded models,* A study conducted on behalf on the National Women's Council of Ireland.

Mc Keown, K. & Fitzgerald, G. (1997), *Developing Childcare Services in Disadvantaged Areas: Final report of the Pilot Childcare Initiative (1994 - 1995).* Dublin: Kieran Mc Keown Ltd.

McKeown, K., Ferguson, H., & Rooney, D. (1998), *Fathers: Irish experience in an international context:* A report to the Commission on the Family.

Mooney, A. & Munton, A.G. (1998), Quality in early childhood services: Parent, provider and policy perspectives, *Children & Society,* 12, 2.

PAUL Partnership, Limerick (1997), *Unpublished Submission to the Expert Working Group on Childcare.*

Penn, H. (1989), Integrating childcare services: Strathclydes's example in I. Williams (ed) *Babies in daycare: an examination of the issues,* London: The Daycare Trust.

Sylva, K. (1995), The impact of early learning on children's later development. In C. Ball (ed), *Start Right: the importance of early learning,* 84 - 96. London: RSA.

United Nations Convention on the Rights of the Child.

Whitebrook, M., Howes, C. & Phillips, D. (1989), *Who cares? Childcare teachers and the quality of care in America*. Final report of the National Child Care Staffing Study.

Williams, J. & Collins, C. (1997) *Childcare arrangements in Ireland: A Report to the Commission on the Family*, Economic and Social Research Institute.

Woodhead, M. (1996), *In search of the rainbow: Pathways to quality in large-scale programmes for young disadvantaged children*. The Hague: Bernard van Leer Foundation.

Membership of the Expert Working Group on Childcare

Chairperson:	Sylda Langford, Assistant Secretary,
	Margaret O'Connor, Principal Officer
Secretary:	Frances Comerford
Secretariat:	Siobhan Barron, Barry Quinn
	Department of Justice, Equality and Law Reform
Operational Support/Advice	Dr. Tony Crooks A.D.M
	Maura Keating
Editorial Advice:	Margaret Kernan C.S.E.R, DIT

Name	**Organisation Represented**
Anderson, Patricia	Waterford Childcare Centre
Beggan, Mary	FÁS
Bernard, Jenny	Council for the West
Boland, Josephine	Teastas
Byrne, Noreen	National Women's Council of Ireland
Byrne, Catherine	Irish National Teachers Organisation (INTO)
Cannon, Anne	Community Playgroup Together
Cashen, Barbara	Employment Equality Agency
Cassidy, Monica	Irish National Organisation for the Unemployed (INOU)
Cassidy, Irene	National Parents Council - Primary
Clarke, Bríd	Health Board
•Tully, Rose/Collins, Jacqueline	National Parents Council -Post Primary
Conway, Linda	FÁS
Crickley, Dr. Anastasia	Platform Against Racism
Crooks, Dr. Tony	Area Development Management Ltd
Cullen, Barry	Children's Centre, Trinity College
•Spillane, Frances /Collins, John	Department of Health and Children
Carey, Eamon	FÁS
Davy, Pauline	Southside Partnership
Deaton, Margaret	European Anti-Pov. Netw. (EAPN) Tallaght Centre
Hegarty, Maria	European Anti-Pov. Netw. (EAPN) Tallaght Centre
Doherty, Margot	TREOIR
Donnelly,Pat	Health Board
Dowdall, Bob	Office of the Revenue Commissioners
Duggan, Siobhan	PLANET - Cork City Partnership
•O Briain, Deaglán/Murphy, Etain /	
Downes, Rosemary/Higgins, Edel	Department of Social, Community & Family Affairs
Fitzpatrick, Siobhan	Northern Ireland Pre-school & Playgroup Assoc. (NIPPA)
Gibbons, Norah	Barnardos
Glackin, Rosaleen	Irish Congress of Trade Unions (ICTU)
Gunning, Irene	Irish Pre-school & Playgroup Assoc.(IPPA)
Gillespie, Ruth/Barron, Joanie	Wallaroo Playschool
Hayes, Nóirín	School of Social Science, DIT
Henson, Marie	Cherish
Healy, Clare	DIT - NOW Childcare Project
Joyce, Chrissie	Irish Traveller Movement (ITM)
Kavanagh, Anne	Sligo County Council

Keane, Cáit/June Hosford	St. Nicholas Montessori Society of Ireland
Killian, Nick	Office of Minister of State
Kearns, Hubert	City and County Managers Association
Keating, Maura	Area Development Management Ltd.
Kenny, Hilary	Irish Pre-school & Playgroup Assoc.(IPPA)
Keogh, Siobhan	Health Board
Lynch, Anna	Focus on Children
•Mulrennan, Madelene/Cullen, Grainne/	
Lynch Orla,	National Council of Vocational Awards (NCVA)
Logue, Andrew	Disability Federation of Ireland (DFI)
Lunny, Leonie	National Social Services Board (NSSB)
Mc Kenna, Dr. Anne	EU Network on Childcare
McElwee, Niall	Waterford Institute of Technology (WIT)
McCormilla, Denise	Border Counties Network
Mc Gowan, Mary	Irish Rural Link
•McGuinness,Annie/McCaffrey,Rose	Cross Border Women's Network
McSweeney, Bríd	Department of Finance
•Gilligan, Paul /Martin, Elaine	Irish Society for the Prevention of Cruelty to Children (ISPCC)
Mullen, Rachel	Women's Aid
Murphy, Martina	National Childrens Nursery Association (NCNA)
•Fitzpatrick, Joan/Murphy, Betty	Irish Farmers Association (IFA)
Murray, Patricia	National Childminding Assoc. of Ireland (NCMAI)
Murray, Colette	Pavee Point
O'Brien, Bríd	Community Workers Co-op
O'Broin, Risteard	Department of Education & Science
O'Connor, Orla	Congress Centres for the Unemployed
O'Connor, Mary	Assoc.for the Welfare of Children in Hospital (Ireland)
O'Donoghue, Aileen	Irish Business & Employers Confederation (IBEC)
O'Farrell, Orlagh	Equal Opportunities DG V (Formerly)
O'Neill, Paula	Tallaght Partnership
O'Regan, Grace	Department of the Taoiseach
O'Shiel, Pearse	Irish Steiner Waldorf Education Association
Parle, Teresa	External Exam Unit - NCVA
Poole, Philomena	Blanchardstown Partnership
Ransom, Janice	One Parent Exchange Network (OPEN)
•Cullen, Paul/ Rawson, Catherine	Dept. Enterprise, Trade and Employment
Ryan, Frances	Irish Vocational Education Association (IVEA)
Ryan, Eamonn	City and County Managers, Association
Ryan, Robbie	IMPACT
Shaw, Anne	Childrens Rights Alliance
•O'Donovan, Adrian /Smith, Kieran	Department of Health and Children
•O'Lionáin Micheál/Stewart, Jacinta	Assoc. of CEO's and VEC's
Uí Ainín, Máire	An Comhchoiste Reamhscolaíochta Teo
Walsh, Deirdre	Department of Health and Children
Zappone, Dr. Katherine	National Womens Council of Ireland

Note: •Indicates changes in representation over the life of the Group

Submissions to the Expert Working Group on Childcare

Muintir Na hÉireann Páirtí Teoranta	The Combat Poverty Agency
Cork College of Commerce	IPPA, Meath Branch
Kerry Diocesan Youth Service	Muintereas Tógra Oideachais Gaeltachta
Positive Action For Children, Co. Cork	Roscommon Pro-Life Pro-Family Group
Eileen O'Sullivan, (International Board Certified Lactation Consultant)	Ronanstown Community Childcare Centre
ASTI	Súgradh
School of Practical Childcare	St. James Hospital, Dublin 8
South Inner City Community Development Association	The Children's Hospital, Temple Street, Dublin 2.
St. Nicholas Montessori College Ireland	The Irish Farmers Association
Community After Schools Project	The Golden Gate Kindergarten Association, USA
The Lifestart Foundation	The National Association for the Welfare of Children
The National Party, Family, Community, Nation	Child and Family Centre
The P.A.U.L. Partnership, Limerick	The Shanty, An Educational Project
Traveller Families Support Service	Treoir, Federation of Services for Unmarried Parents and their Children
The Women's Centre	Environmental Health Officers Association
Carlow Institute of Further Education	Naíonra Lios Na nÓg
Early Childhood Training Project	S.I.P.T.U
National Co-Op Farm Relief Services Ltd	Cara Park Training Centre Ltd
City of Helsinki Social Services Department	Teagasc
Women's Education Research and Resource Centre	Access 2000
Naíonra Gaelscoil an Teaghlaigh Naofa	Ballymun Partnership
Breslin International Recruitment	Brothers of Charity Services
Childcare Network - Loch Garman	Childcare Special Interest Group, Dundalk
Childcare Special Interest Group	Childcare Special Interest Group
Childcare Support Group, Co. Laois	Combat Poverty Agency
County Sligo Leader Partnership Company	Early Childhood Training Project, Galway
Community Play-Groups Together in Greater Dublin area and South Side Dublin	Cork Early Years Network
Naíonra Community Playgroup	County Wexford Partnership, Enniscorthy
Dublin City Wide Drugs Crisis Campaign	D.I.T. New Opportunities for Women
Féach	Family Alert, Waterford
Inner City Organisation Network	Foróige - National Youth Development Organisation
Irish Congress of Trade Unions	Irish Association of Social Workers

Jungle Box Childcare Centre, Co. Wexford

Labour Women's National Council
Lifestart Lifford/Clonleigh, Co.Donegal
National Educational Council, Co. Waterford

National Rehabilitation Board
Parents Alone Resource Centre
Sligo Social Service Council Ltd.
Wexford Area Partnership
Women's Network, Clondalkin
Tallaght Partnership
Clarecare
The Royal College of Psychiatrists
Naíonra Bhearna
Cosaint na Beatha agus an Teaghlaigh
Naíonra Chnoc Liamhna
Naíonra Naomh Iosaf
Coiste na dTuismitheoirí

Eigse Dún Dealgan
Waterford Institute of Technology

C.O.R.I. - Justice Committee

National Childminders Union
Western Health Board

Irish Steiner Schools Association
Knockanrawley Resource Centre Ltd.,
Co.Tipperary
Lifestart Family Centre, Co.Sligo
Moatview Day Nursery, Dublin 12
Network - The Organisation for Women in
Business
One Parent Exchange and Network
Second Chance Education Project for Women
Support Life Ireland
Wexford Women's Action Group
Women in the Home
Newbury House Family Centre
Cherry Orchard Council
Planet Network
Comhluadar
Naíonra Ceatharlach agus Asca
Na Naíonraí Gaelacha
Naíonra an Daingin
Castletownbere Community Playgroup and
Day Nursery Ltd
An Comhchoiste Reamhscolaíochta Teo
Dept. of Education - National Education for
Travellers
Mornington Heights Residents Association,
Co.Meath

Thirty four submissions were received from individuals and parents nationwide including:
Donal O'Driscoll
Gabriel Fleming
Marie Oswald Caffrey
Mary Stewart
Padraig Hunt
Lelia O'Flaherty
Anne Crowley
Margaret O'Regan
Kathleen Lavin
Joseph Neylon
Mary T. Geever

Terms of Reference of the subgroups of the Expert Working Group on Childcare - Established October '97

Group 1 :

The financial and employment implications of an integrated approach to the provision of childcare services in Ireland

The core aim of this '*Framework Development Group*' is to estimate the broad financial implications of an integrated approach to the provision of childcare services in Ireland. This will incorporate particular attention to quantifying the job potential of the childcare sector. The group will explore practical solutions to overcome barriers to maximising full development of services and personnel for the sector.

Specific objectives

1. Consider the conclusions of the Working Group on the Job Potential of Childcare and the ESRI survey of childcare arrangements being undertaken on behalf of the Commission on the Family.

2. Estimate the extent of childcare provision at present.

3. Assess the demand for childcare services.

4. Examine the effect on supply and demand of bringing all childcare provision into the formal economy.

5. Consider the implications/benefits of providing:
   (a) Tax relief to parents availing of childcare
   (b) State subsidies to childcare facilities.

6. Examine appropriate rates of pay for childcare workers in co-operation with the Registration, Training and Qualifications subgroup.

7. Develop a framework/strategy which nurtures the appropriate environment to enable growth in terms of secure, recognised employment and career structures in childcare.

8. Integrate the costings of childcare provisions in rural and disadvantaged areas (from respective sub groups) into the overall framework for financing the childcare sector.

The group should also take account of:
- Ways to develop support for the private, self-employed, the public and community/co-op sectors in their provision of childcare services.

- The potential of childcare enterprises as social enterprises which could attract support from public funds.

- The economics for families of availing of childcare services.

- A commitment to pursue a policy of equality of access and participation.

Membership

Dr. Katherine Zappone, Chair	NWCI
Patricia Murray, Deputy Chair	NMAI
Barbara Cashen	E.E.A
Pauline Davy	Sth.side Partnership
Aileen O'Donoghue	IBEC
Paul Cullen/ Catherine Rawson	Dept. Enterprise, Trade & Employment
Denise McCormilla	Border Counties N.
Margaret Deaton / Maria Hegarty	E.A.P.N
Mary Beggan	FÁS
Martina Murphy	NCNA
Bob Dowdall	Rev. Comm
Adrian O'Donovan / Kieran Smith	Dept. Health and Children

Group 2:

Registration, Training and Qualifications'

The core aim of this *'Framework Development Group'* is to explore practical solutions to overcome barriers in relation to registration, training and qualifications within the childcare sector. Specific objectives:

Registration:

1 Establish what is the desirable best practice in the development of a national registration system for all childcarers.

2. Consider the implications of developing a national registration system.

3. Explore the potential of a system of provision of information on registered carers and facilities for parents.

Training and Qualifications:

1. Examine the levels of training and qualifications required for the different positions with the employment market.

2. Explore models of accreditation of prior learning and propose appropriate ways of achieving this in childcare.

3. Examine a means of bringing childcare and early education into a cohesive and integrated whole to allow interaction among family, childcare and school systems.

4. Identify what is desirable best practice in student placement on vocational education and training programmes.

5. Propose a framework, guiding principles, methodology for the co-ordination of the delivery of childcare training, taking account of the need for flexibility and accessibility.

The group should also take account of:

- A commitment to pursue a policy of equality of access and participation.

Membership

Rosaleen Glackin Chair	ICTU
Michéal O'Lionáin/ Jacinta Stewart	Assoc. of CEOs of VECs
Deirdre Walsh	Dept. Health & Children
Monica Cassidy	INOU
Linda Conway/	
Eamonn Carey	FÁS
Cáit Keane/June Hosford	St. Nicholas Montessori Soc. of Ireland
Madelaine Mulrennan/	
Grainne Cullen / Orla Lynch	NCVA
Clare Healy	DIT/NOW Project
Irene Gunning	IPPA
Noreen Byrne	NWCI
Josephine Boland	Teastas
Risteard O'Broin	Dept. of Education & Science
Niall McElwee	WIT
Catherine Byrne	INTO
Robbie Ryan	IMPACT

Group 3 :
'Resourcing and sustaining childcare within urban disadvantaged areas'

The core aim of this *'Framework Development Group'* is to explore practical solutions to overcome the barriers to resourcing and sustaining childcare within urban disadvantaged areas.

Specific objectives:

1. Carry out a cost/benefit analysis of State support for childcare and of State support for particularly vulnerable groups in disadvantaged urban areas.

2. Examine the role and contribution of all key statutory agencies in providing support for childcare in urban disadvantaged areas.

3. Examine the potential role and contribution of the private sector (i.e. business and employers) as it relates to disadvantaged urban areas.

4. Examine the role and contribution of the voluntary and community sector in providing support for childcare in urban disadvantaged areas.

5. Explore and develop practical strategies to promote long-term sustainability of childcare in urban disadvantaged areas.

6. Develop a framework to enable and encourage access to affordable, high quality childcare services in disadvantaged urban areas.

The group should also take account of:

- A commitment to pursue a policy of equality of access and participation.

- Models of good practice and how they can be replicated.

- Community involvement in the delivery of childcare services and identify support mechanisms for community based initiatives.

Membership

Hilary Kenny, Chair	IPPA
Philomena Poole, Deputy Chair	Blanchardstown Partnership
Siobhan Fitzpatrick	NIPPA
Grace O'Regan	Dept.An Taoiseach
Siobhan Duggan	PLANET
Deaglán O'Briain/ Etain Murphy/ Rosemary Downes/ Edel Higgins	Dept.Social Community & Family Affairs
Janice Ransom	OPEN
Bríd McSweeney	Dept. of Finance
Paula O'Neill	Tallaght Partnership
Bríd Clarke	Health Board
Ann Cannon	Community Playgroups Together
Mary O'Connor	Assoc. for Welfare Children in Hospital (Ire)
Eamonn Ryan	City & County Managers Association
Pearse O'Shiel	Irish Steiner Waldorf Education Assoc.

Group 4:

'Resourcing and sustaining childcare within rural areas'.

The core aim of this *'Framework Development Group'* is to explore practical solutions to overcome the barriers to resourcing and sustaining childcare within rural areas.

Specific objectives:

1. Carry out a cost/benefit analysis of State support for childcare and of State support for particularly vulnerable groups in rural areas.

2. Examine the role and contribution of local authorities and health boards in providing support for childcare.

3. Examine the potential role and contribution of the private sector as it relates to rural areas.

4. Explore and develop practical strategies to promote long-term sustainability of childcare in rural areas.

5. Develop a framework to encourage access to affordable, high quality childcare services in rural areas.

The group should also take account of:

- The childcare needs of parents in rural areas and in particular the childcare needs of lone parents and those in isolated areas.

- Community involvement in the delivery of childcare services and identify support mechanisms for community based initiatives.

- Appropriate childcare facilities that take account of rural diversity and diversity of needs.

- A means to co-ordinate childcare services in rural areas.

- Models of good practice and how they can be replicated.

- A commitment to pursue a policy of equality of access and participation.

Membership

Pat Donnelly, Chair	Health Board CEO Representative
Jenny Bernard, Deputy Chair	Council for the West
Frances Ryan	IVEA
Máire Uí Ainín	An Comhchoiste Reamhscolaíochta Teo
Joan Fitzpatrick/ Betty Murphy	IFA
Mary McGowan	Irish Rural Link
Annie McGuinness/ Rose McCaffrey	Cross Border Women's Network
Hubert Kearns	County & City Man. Assoc
Dr. Anne Mc Kenna	EU Network on Childcare
Anne Kavanagh	Sligo County Council

Group 5:

'Regulations and Standards'

The core aim of this *'Framework Development Group'* is to explore practical solutions to overcome the barriers to development which have been identified.

Specific objectives

1. To monitor the implementations of the Child Care (Pre-School Services) Regulations, 1996 and Part VII of the Child Care Act, 1991.

2. To provide a forum for dealing with practice issues on a national basis.

3. To ensure standardisation in the approach of health boards to the Regulations.

4. To report to the Expert Working Group on Childcare established under Partnership 2000.

Membership

Frances Spillane/ John Collins, Chair	Dept. Health & Children
Deirdre Walsh, Deputy Chair	Dept Health & Children
Brid Clarke	Eastern Health Board
Dorothy Mangan	Midland Health Board
Ger Crowley	Mid-Western Health Board
Pat Donnelly	North Eastern Health Board
Val O'Kelly	North Western Health Board
Ann Boyle	South Eastern Health Board
Bernadette Cahill	Southern Health Board
James Mansfield	Western Health Board
Adrian O'Donovan	Dept. Health & Children
Siobhan Phelan	Dept.Health & Children

Group 6 :

'Early Education' *

The main focus of this subgroup was to discuss and highlight the educational nature of high quality childcare. The Core Aim of the subgroup was:- to explore practical solutions to overcoming barriers to recognising the educational nature of high quality childcare. **Specific objectives:-**

1. To review the ways in which development of early services internationally recognise the educational nature of childcare.

2. To prepare the Working Group submission to the National Forum on Early Childhood Education.

3. To monitor the progress of the National Forum.

4. To consider the Report of the National Forum.

5. To report to the Expert Working Group.

Membership	
Noirin Hayes, Chair	DIT
Hilary Kenny	IPPA
Risteard O'Broin	Dept. of Education & Science
Pat Donnelly	Health Board
Andrew Logue	Disability Fed of Ireland
Denise McCormilla	Border Counties Network
Elaine Martin	ISPCC

*This subgroup was not formed until January, 1998.

Group 7:

'The needs and rights of children in relation to a national framework'

The core aim of this *'Framework Resource Group'* is to provide guiding principles on the needs and rights of children which can underpin the development of a national framework.

Specific objectives:

1. Devise guiding principles to inform, feed andhelp focus the strategies of the *'Framework Development Groups'*.

2. Devise a common statement of agreement on the needs and rights of children in relation to a national framework.

In doing so, the group should take account of the following:

- How to encourage a safe, secure and high quality environment for children availing of childcare services.

- How to ensure that children's needs for stimulation and educational development are met.

- The supports required for childcare facilities to comply with Section VII of the Child Care Act, 1991.

- The adequacy of existing procedures for clearance of childcare workers.

- How to encourage equality of access for all children 0 - 12 years.

- The needs of specific groups of children and how those needs can best be met - e.g. children whose behaviour presents a particular challenge, children with a disability, Traveller children.

- A means of bringing childcare and early education into a cohesive and integrated whole to allow interactions among family, childcare and school systems.

- The most appropriate staffing structure to ensure children benefit as much as possible.

- A commitment to pursue a policy of equality of access and participation.

Membership

Norah Gibbons, Chair	Barnardos
Paul Gilligan/ Elaine Martin, Deputy Chair	ISPCC
Marie Henson	Cherish
Siobhan Keogh	Health Board
Irene Cassidy	Nat. Parents Co. Primary
Anna Lynch	Focus on Children
Anne Shaw	Children's Rights Alliance
Rose Tully/ Jacqueline Collins	National Parents Co. Post Primary
Patricia Anderson	Waterford Childcare Centre
Leonie Lunny	NSSB

Group 8:

'Equality of access and participation in relation to a national framework'

The core aim of this *'Framework Resource Group'* is to provide guiding principles on equality of access and participation which can resource and underpin the development of a national framework.

Specific objectives.

1. Devise guiding principles to inform, feed and help focus the strategies of the 'Framework Development Groups'.

2. Devise a common statement of agreement on equality of access and participation in relation to a national framework.

3. Devise a strategy to promote equal opportunities in childcare services and training.

4. Identify the National Policy options that would contribute to promoting equality in childcare services.

In doing so, the group should take account of the following:
- The economics for low income families of availing of childcare services.

- The most equitable way to provide State financial support to ensure that those most in need benefit.

- The need to encourage access to affordable, high quality childcare services in disadvantaged urban areas.

- The value of childcare training and practice which is non-discriminatory, inclusive and intercultural.

- Childcare as a means to promote equal opportunities and social inclusion, and as a means to break the cycle of disadvantage.

- The needs of specific groups of children and how those needs can best be met - e.g. children whose behaviour presents a particular challenge, children with a disability, Traveller children.

- Consider and make recommendations regarding the organisation of working time and its impact on families.

Membership:

Orla O'Connor, Chair	Congress Centres for the Unemployed
Brid O'Brien, Deputy Chair Comm.Wkr.Co.op	I.T.M.
Chrissie Joyce	
Andrew Logue	D.F.I.
Orlagh O'Farrell	Eq.Opps DGV
Teresa Parle	Extern/ NCVA
Ruth Gillespie/	Wallaroo Plygp
Joanie Barron	
Colette Murray	Pavee Point
Nick Killian	Office Minister of State
Barry Cullen	Children's CentreTrinity
Dr. Anastasia Crickley	Platform Against Racism
Margot Doherty	Treoir
Rachel Mullen	Women's Aid

Presentation on behalf of the Expert Working Group on Childcare to the National Forum on Early Education 24 March 1998

Background

We are here to make a presentation on behalf of the Expert Working Group on Childcare which was established under Partnership 2000 to devise a national framework for the development and delivery of childcare and early educational services in Ireland, in the context of promoting equality, particularly equal opportunities in employment.

In order to develop a national framework, the Expert Working Group are considering a range of issues:

- the financial and employment implications of an integrated approach to the development of childcare facilities in Ireland
- registration, training and qualifications for childcare workers
- resourcing and sustaining childcare within urban disadvantaged areas
- resourcing and sustaining childcare within rural areas
- the needs and rights of children in relation to a national framework
- equality of access and participation in relation to a national framework
- early education

The early education subgroup was set up to address the educational nature of childcare. The core aim of the group is **to explore practical solutions to overcoming barriers to recognising the educational nature of high quality childcare** and to provide a link between the Expert Group and this Forum.

In addition, a group monitoring the implementation of Part VII of the Child Care Act in relation to standards and regulations for certain pre-school services, is feeding into the Expert Working Group.

There are over 70 members, representing a range of Government departments, statutory bodies, non-governmental organisations, users and service providers who have an expertise and interest in the childcare area.

We represent the Secretariat of the Expert Group, which is based in the Department of Justice, Equality and Law Reform.

Submission

The Expert Working Group welcomes the terms of reference of this Forum, particularly the age range of 0 to 6 years. The Expert Group's remit is children aged 0 - 12 years.

The Expert Group believes that children learn from birth and that parents are their first teachers. As such, parents should be supported in their role by a variety of different means geared to meeting the needs of children and parents. Indeed, society should share this responsibility with parents.

The Expert Group urges the Forum to encourage the development of mechanisms to strengthen supports for parents.

The issues I will cover today include:
- Encouragement and support for parents in their role as educators
- Early childhood services
- Curriculum
- Collaboration between systems and actors
- Resources and mechanisms
- Quality and Equality
- Partnership as the way forward

1. Recognise and support the role of parents

Role of Parents / Partnership

Parents are the first educators of their children and active partners in the continuing process of education. Parental involvement does not merely contribute to quality but is essential if early education is to be successful.

The role of parents in the education of their children needs to be supported. This could be achieved through partnership facilitating dialogue and the sharing of expertise and information.

As a child moves from the close relationship of family life into a new situation such as a childcare/early education service, the close involvement of parents can supply both important continuity for the child and information for the educator. In planning to fulfil objectives in the education of children under the age of six, the starting point must be the needs and characteristics of the child and these can be assessed by collaboration with parents.

Establishing a partnership with the home provides a firm foundation on which subsequent educators can build in the child's interest. It is important that services with which parents are happy evolve and this can best be achieved in partnership with parents.

The elements necessary for successful parental involvement include consultation and negotiation in relation to matters such as structure, conditions and hours, parental familiarity with the programme or curriculum and regular reports on children's progress.

It is important that parents are facilitated so that they can make an informed choice about what is the best childcare and education for their children through information, advice and openness.

Mechanisms

It is important to consider mechanisms for facilitating regular consultation and collaboration between the different systems involved in the early education of young children at national, regional and local levels.

The Expert Group has not completed its consideration of appropriate structures, but it is apparent that there must be co-operation between all the actors, at all levels. Policies must be 'child proofed' to ensure that the needs of children are met in a co-ordinated way. Co-operation between policy makers at national level must be complimented by regional and local mechanisms that facilitate involvement of all interested parties and liaison at the point of delivery of services.

Resources

Costing and realistic resourcing of mechanisms to support parents, communities, providers and policy makers involved in the early education of children must be tackled. Time and resources invested can pay rich dividends in terms of the attitudes of parents and children to learning, the emotional development of children, their socialisation, the growth of confidence and independence, which are important tools in combating abuse, the identification of problems at an early stage and prevention of future difficulties. Resources provided for the development of good systems and support for families should be regarded as an investment in the future of children and the country.

2. Early Education / Childcare

Early childhood services

The Expert Group endorses the background paper prepared for the Forum and considers that is neither possible nor valuable to separate out the educational and care elements of early childhood services. Care and education for the under sixes are complementary and inseparable.

In the early stages of its work the Expert Working Group discussed the term "childcare" in detail, particularly the relationship between care and education. The agreed definition describes day-care facilities and services for pre-school children and school-going children out of school hours.

It includes services offering care, education and socialisation opportunities for children, to the benefit of children, parents, employers and the wider community. Thus services such as pre-schools, naíonraí, day-care services, crèches, playgroups, private childminding and after-school groups are included but schools (i.e. primary, secondary and special schools) and residential centres for children are excluded.

The Expert Group believes that the value of early childhood services in meeting, not only the needs of children and their families, but also the community and society in general must be recognised. The community benefits from the drawing of people into groups working together. Society benefits from the opportunities presented to children to develop social skills, sharing, interaction with others, opportunities which are not always available otherwise, given demographic, societal and family changes.

There is a need to redefine childcare as a universal system of value in itself in the same way as the primary and secondary educational system is currently recognised.

Research has shown that social and life skills learned in the pre-school environment remain with the child. It is therefore in the child's interest that early education should be focused on emotional, social, cognitive and physical development.

Curriculum

The Working Group understands that the Primary curriculum is currently under review. We urge the Forum to look carefully at the concept of curriculum in the context of quality early education provision.

A curriculum has been defined as all things that happen to children. Everything children see, hear, do and their interaction with their environment form part of the curriculum and it is important to look at curriculum in its widest meaning.

The curriculum developed for children under age 6 should acknowledge that children require care and support in their cognitive, social and emotional development. It should thus include play-based education and quality controls.

Play is a good deal more than recreation and if well planned has a fundamental role in early childhood education. Young children are social beings and learning should take place in a social context.

The Expert Group recommends curriculum guidelines which take the approach of the wider concept of curriculum, with guidelines around best practice, innovative work and how children learn, regardless of the sector in which early education is being provided.

Learning should be a pleasurable and rewarding experience. A curriculum should recognise that every child is unique. Young children's development should be viewed as a whole and the curriculum should reflect an understanding of this. Effective curriculum planning and implementation requires common and clearly understood aims, objectives and values. Curriculum planning is a continuous cycle involving planning, observation, recording and assessment.

All those involved in the learning process should be viewed as partners and should collaborate in planning the curriculum. This includes policy makers, parents and providers.

Quality and Equality

A quality early childhood service is one that offers both care and educational opportunities appropriate to the individual child's age and stage of development and provides equal opportunities for all children attending. As such it requires a quality environment which offers appropriate equipment and materials. It also requires that the adults involved are aware of children's needs and have the necessary skills and attitudes which are important in terms of their interaction with children, parents and other personnel. Quality also requires regular access to in-service training.

Quality early years services benefit individual children, individual families and the community and enable the educational system itself to function better in meeting its own objectives.

The role of quality early childhood services in promoting equal opportunities is fundamental to the work of the Expert Group.

The Group is committed to a policy of equality of access and participation in relation to the development of a national framework. As referred to earlier, the Group is considering access in terms of disadvantaged areas and communities from both urban and rural perspectives whilst recognising the needs and rights of children, including children with disabilities and special needs, Traveller children and children from diverse cultural backgrounds.

The role of quality childcare services in enabling parents to access employment, training, educational and social opportunities is central to the Group's work.

The Group believes that equality of access and opportunity and the needs and rights of children must be the main focus of a national framework.

Choice and partnership

There is no single early educational service that will meet the needs of all children at different ages, those living in different locations or in different circumstances. Parents should be encouraged so that they can make an informed choice in relation to the type of services available and whether they wish to avail of those services for their children.

The Expert Group notes the well developed systems of partnership emerging and urges the Forum to encourage the development of partnerships at all levels, including national, regional and local. It also urges the Forum to identify and operationally define mechanisms to support true partnership in any early education service. This partnership will vary depending on the age of the child, the service in question and the circumstances of parents.

Conclusion

In conclusion, the Expert Working Group welcomes the Department of Education and Science acknowledgement that learning and education start at birth and that parents have a vital role to play as the child's first educator. The Group believes that parents should be supported in that role and that society shares responsibility with parents for education and development of children.

Partnership can take many forms and the Expert Group encourages the development of mechanisms to strengthen and support the role of parents in partnership at all levels. The Group endorses the development of different systems and wishes to encourage collaboration between these systems. It is important that service providers and policy makers work in co-operation with parents and do not work in isolation from each other.

And so, on behalf of the Expert Working Group, I would like to thank you for this opportunity to present the Group's thinking on issues which it considers important to this Forum and to thank you for the opportunity to participate in, and influence the process.

The Group awaits your report with interest and will take your conclusions into consideration when drawing up its own report.

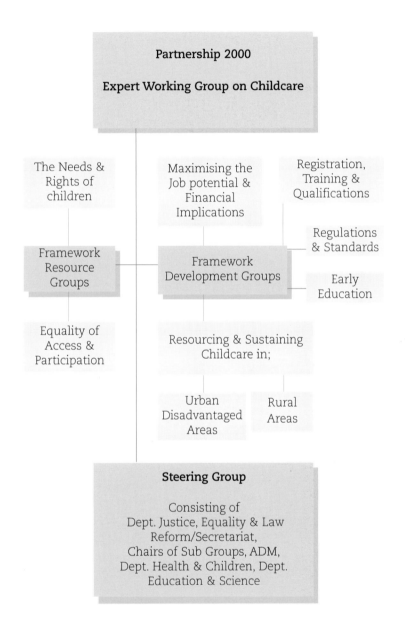

Partnership 2000

Expert Working Group on Childcare

The Needs & Rights of children

Maximising the Job potential & Financial Implications

Registration, Training & Qualifications

Framework Resource Groups

Framework Development Groups

Regulations & Standards

Early Education

Equality of Access & Participation

Resourcing & Sustaining Childcare in;

Urban Disadvantaged Areas

Rural Areas

Steering Group

Consisting of
Dept. Justice, Equality & Law Reform/Secretariat,
Chairs of Sub Groups, ADM,
Dept. Health & Children, Dept. Education & Science

Research reports commissioned by the Expert Working Group on Childcare

Consultation with Children and Parents (Fingleton, M., February, 1998).

Research on Guidelines for Minimum Standards for Registration of Childcare Facilities (National Children's Resource Centre, Barnardo's, March 1998).

Identification of Training Needs of the Childcare Sector(Centre for Social and Educational Research (CSER), Dublin Institute of Technology, March 1998).

Study of Family Day Care (Childminding) Provision, (Centre for Social and Educational Research (CSER), Dublin Institute of Technology, June 1998).

The Economics of Childcare in Ireland (Goodbody Economic Consultants in association with The Economic and Social Research Institute, the Department of Psychology, University College, Dublin and The Policy Studies Institute, UK, October, 1998).

These research reports will be made available by the Department of Justice, Equality and Law Reform.

Quality Targets in Services for Young Children European, Commission Network on Childcare, January 1996 Proposals for a ten year action programme

TARGET 1: Governments should draw on professional and public opinion to provide a published and coherent statement of intent for care and education services to young children 0-6, in the public and in the private sector, at national and at regional/local level. This policy should set out principles, specify objectives and define priorities, and explain how such initiatives will be co-ordinated between relevant departments.

TARGET 2: At national level one department should be nominated to take responsibility for implementing the policy whether it does so directly or through an agency; at a regional/local level there should be a similar designation of responsibility, whether services are directly administered by the regional/local authority or whether contracted out to other providers.

TARGET 3: Governments should draw up a programme to implement the policy which outlines strategies for implementation, sets targets and specifies resources. At a regional/local level, the department or agency responsible should similarly draw up a programme for implementing policy and developing practice.

TARGET 4: Legislative frameworks should be created to ensure that the targets are fully met within specified time limits and reviewed regularly, and should outline the competencies of regional and/or local government in fulfilling the targets.

TARGET 5: The Government department or agency responsible at national level should set up an infrastructure, with parallel structures at local level, for planning, monitoring, review, support, training, research and service development.

TARGET 6: The planning and monitoring system should include measures of supply, demand and need covering all services for young children at national, regional and/or local level.

TARGET 7: Public expenditure on services for young children (in this case defined as children aged 5 years and under) should be not less than 1% of GDP in order to meet targets set for services, both for children under three and over three.

TARGET 8: A proportion of this budget should be allocated to develop the infrastructure for services. This should include at least 5% spent on support and advisory services including continuous or in-service training and at least 1% for research and monitoring.

TARGET 9: There should be a capital spending programme for building and renovations linked to the environmental and health targets.

TARGET 10: Where parents pay for publicly funded services, the charges should not exceed, and may well be less than, 15% of net monthly household income. The charges should take into account per capita income, family size and other relevant circumstances.

TARGET 11: Publicly funded services should offer full time equivalent places for:

- at least 90% of children aged 3-6 years; and
- at least 15% of children under three years.

TARGET 12: Services should offer flexibility of hours and attendance including coverage for working hours and a working year if parents require it.

TARGET 13: There should be a range of services offering parents choice.

TARGET 14: All services should positively assert the value of diversity and make provision both for children and adults which acknowledges and supports diversity of language, ethnicity, religion, gender and disability, and challenges stereotypes.

TARGET 15: All children with disabilities should have right of access to the same services as other children with appropriate staffing assistance and specialist help.

TARGET 16: All collective services for young children 0-6 whether in the public or private sector should have coherent values and objectives including a stated and explicit educational philosophy.

TARGET 17: The educational philosophy should be drawn up and developed by parents, staff and other interested groups.

TARGET 18: The educational philosophy should be broad and include and promote inter alia:

- the child's autonomy and concept of self
- convivial social relationships between children, and children and adults
- a zest for learning
- linguistic and oral skills including linguistic diversity
- mathematical, biological, scientific, technical and environmental concepts musical expression and aesthetic skills
- drama, puppetry and mime
- muscular co-ordination and bodily control
- health, hygiene, food and nutrition
- awareness of the local community.

TARGET 19: The way in which the educational philosophy is put into practice should be stated and explicit. Services should have a programme of organisation covering all their activities including pedagogical approach, deployment of staff, grouping of children, training profiles for staff, use of space, and the way in which financial resources are used to implement the programme.

TARGET 20: The education and learning environment should reflect and value each child's family, home, language, cultural heritage, beliefs, religion and gender.

TARGET 21: Staff ratios for collective care should reflect the objectives of the service and their wider context and be directly related to group age and group size. They should usually be more than but should not be less than:

- 1 adult: 4 places for children aged 12 months
- 1 adult: 6 places for children aged 12-23 months
- 1 adult: 8 places for children aged 24-35 months
- 1 adult: 15 places for children aged 36-71 months

Ratios in family day care should not be less than 1 adult: 4 places for children under compulsory school age, and the ratio should include the family day carer's own children.

TARGET 22: At least one tenth of the working week should be non-contact time allocated to preparation and continuous training.

TARGET 23: Adequate supply cover should always be available to maintain the ratios.

TARGET 24: Administrative, domestic and janitorial work should be allocated staff time or hours in addition to those hours spent with children.

TARGET 25: All qualified staff employed in services should be paid at not less than a nationally or locally agreed wage rate, which for staff who are fully trained should be comparable to that of teachers.

TARGET 26: A minimum of 60% of staff working directly with children in collective services should have a grant eligible basic training of at least three years at a post 18 level, which incorporates both the theory and practice of pedagogy and child development. All training should be modular. All staff in services (both collective and family day care) who are not trained to this level should have right of access to such training, including on an in-service basis.

TARGET 27: All staff in services working with children (in both collective and family day care) should have the right to continuous in-service training.

TARGET 28: All staff whether in the public or the private sector shall have the right to trade union affiliation.

TARGET 29: 20% of staff employed in collective services should be men.

TARGET 30: All services, whether in the private or the public sector, should meet national and local health and safety requirements.

TARGET 31: The planning of the environment and its spatial organization, including the layout of the buildings, the furnishings and equipment should reflect the educational philosophy of the service and take account of the views of parents, staff and other interested parties.

TARGET 32: There should normally be sufficient space, inside and out, to enable children to play, sleep and use bathroom facilities, and to meet the needs of parents and staff. This should normally mean:

- internal space of at least 6 sq. metres for each child under three years and of at least 4 sq. metres for each child 3-6 years (excluding storage and corridor or through-way space)
- direct access to external space of at least 6 sq. metres per child
- an additional 5% of internal space for adult use.

TARGET 33: Food preparation facilities should be available on the premises and nutritional and culturally appropriate food should be provided.

TARGET 34: Parents are collaborators and participants in early years services. As such they have a right to give and receive information and the right to express their views both formal and informally. The decision making processes of the services should be fully participative, involving parents, all staff, and where possible, children.

TARGET 35: Services should have formal and informal links with the local community or communities or district.

TARGET 36: Services should adopt employment procedures which emphasize the importance of recruiting employees who reflect the ethnic diversity of the local community.

TARGET 37: Services should demonstrate how they are fulfilling their aims and objectives and how they have spent their budget, through an annual report or by other means.

TARGET 38: In all services children's progress should be regularly assessed.

TARGET 39: The views of parents and the wider community should be an integral part of the assessment process.

TARGET 40: Staff should regularly assess their performance, using both objective methods and self-evaluation. Appendix 5.1

Articles of the UN Convention on the Rights of the Child as referred to in this Report.

Summary of reports, legislation, and initiatives in the area of childcare in Ireland between 1980 and 1998[1]

Name of Body Undertaking Study or Initiative	Date of Publication or Establishment	Appointing Body /Dept	Summary
Task Force on Childcare Services	1980	Department of Health	Primary focus of Task force was on the extension and improvement of services for deprived children and children at risk.
Working Party on Childcare Facilities for Working Parents	1982	Department of Labour	Recommended that Department of Health should have overall responsibility for childcare services and an independent National Childcare Authority should be appointed by the Department of Health with representatives from other Government Departments.
Working Party on Women's Affairs and Family Law Reform	1985	Department of An Taoiseach	Brief was to consider the best administrative measures to promote positive opportunities and facilities to enable women to participate more fully in the life of the community. Recommended a system of registration for child care facilities based on minimum prescribed standards, an expansion of work-based childcare facilities, making child care expenses of parents offsetable against income tax.
Committee on Minimum Legal Requirements and Standards for Day Care Services	1985	Department of Health	Recommended introduction of a compulsory registration system of childcare facilities. Also recommended that through the health boards, a new position Area Organiser/co-ordinator for Day Care Services should be established in each Community Care Area to co-ordinate, support and oversee provision of childcare facilities

Name of Body Undertaking Study or Initiative	Date of Publication or Establishment	Appointing Body/Dept	Summary
National Economic & Social Study on Women's Participation in the Irish Labour Market	1991	NESC	Called for the development of an overall national policy on childcare for working parents - this would be "the single most important policy to facilitate labour force participation by married women" (Callan & Farrell, 1991 pp.8-9).
Report of the Second Commission on the Status of Women	1993	Department of Equality and Law Reform	Considered childcare from the twin perspectives of gender equality in the labour market and child protection and development. Recommendations included: the appointment of childcare co-ordinator in every health board, the need for a system to ensure minimally adequate standards in childcare facilities, properly accredited training for all childcare workers and the development of workplace childcare facilities in larger organisations. Dept. of Equality and Law Reform is responsible for assessing the recommendations of this Commission and drawing up more detailed proposals for action.
Working Group on Childcare Facilities for Working Parents	1994	Department of Equality & Law Reform	Report identified the "current absence of a national strategy for the general development of childcare provision" and to a lesser extent, "the fragmentation of responsibility for child care issues at the level of Government" as the principal reasons for inadequate provision of childcare facilities (Working Group on Childcare Facilities for Working Parents, 1994, pp.3-4).
Evaluation of the Pilot Childcare Initiative	1997	Department of Equality and Law Reform	This initiative (1994-1995) was an initiative of the Dept. of Equality and Law Reform which involved the expenditure on Childcare of IR£2.7 million towards

Name of Body Undertaking Study or Initiative	Date of Publication or Establishment	Appointing Body/Dept.	Summary
			the provision of childcare facilities in disadvantaged areas for the purpose of facilitating the participation of socially excluded parents in employment, training or education. The initiative was designed and implemented by Area Development Management Limited (ADM). The Initiative was extended in 1998 with a budgetary allocation of IR£3.6 million p.a. It is now called the Equal Opportunities Childcare Programme.
United Nations Convention on the Rights of the Child: First National Report of Ireland	1996	Department of Foreign Affairs	The UN Committee on the Rights of the Child is an inter national body of child rights experts which has been established to monitor the implementation of the Convention. The First National Report of Ireland was submitted by the Irish Government to the UN Committee. Examination of this Report took place during Ireland's plenary session with the UN Committee in Geneva, in January 1998.
Partnership 2000 for Inclusion Employment and Competitiveness	1996	Department of an Taoiseach	Expert Working Group on Childcare was established under the Partnership 2000 agreement, to devise a National Framework for the Development of the Childcare Sector.
Child Care (Pre-School Services) Regulations, Part VII of Child Care Act (1991)	1996	Department of Health	Part VII of the Child Care Act places a statutory duty on health boards to secure the health, safety, and welfare and to promote the development of pre-school children attending pre-school services. The

Name of Body Undertaking Study or Initiative	Date of Publication or Establishment	Appointing BodyDept.	Summary
			Regulations require adherence to minimum standards with regard to safety, premises, facilities and maintenance of records.
Small Voices: Vital Rights: Submission to the UN Committee on the Rights of the Child by the Children's Rights Alliance.	1997	Children's Rights Alliance	The submission represents the views of the Children's Rights Alliance on how Irish law, policy and practice comply with the principles and standards of the Convention and identifies the further measures it considers necessary to ensure compliance.
National Forum for Early Childhood Education	1998	Department of Education and Science	National Forum took place in March 1998. It provided an opportunity for all interested groups to engage in a full exchange of views and for each group to put forward their own particular concerns and objectives towards the development of a national framework for early childhood education. The Report of the National Forum was published in November 1998. A White Paper on Early Education is due to be published by May 1999 which will cover issues such as funding, certification, curriculum and co-ordination.
Equal Opportunities Childcare Programme	1998	Department of Justice, Equality and Law Reform	This programme which is being managed by ADM in conjunction with Dept. Justice, Equality and Law Reform contains 3 funding initiatives: Capital Infrastructure Childcare Initiative, Employer Demonstration Childcare Initiative and Community Support Childcare Initiative. All three initiatives are interdependent and strive towards the common aim of improving the quality and quantity of childcare provision in Ireland from an equal opportunities/disadvantaged perspective.

Name of Body Undertaking Study or Initiative	Date of Publication or Establihment	Appointing BodyDept.	Summary
Report of Commission on the Family 'Strengthening Families for Life'	1998	Department of Social, Community and Family Affairs	The brief was to examine the needs and priorities of families in the fast changing social and economic environment. Recommended an approach to supporting families in carrying out their functions which: prioritises investment in the care of young children, supports parents' choices in the care and education of their children, provides practical support and recognition to those who undertake the main caring responsibilities for children, facilitates families in balancing work commitments and family life.

1 Much of the information presented in Table 1.1 was sourced in McKeown & Fitzgerald (1997) Final Report of the Pilot Childcare Initiative (1994-1995) Developing Childcare Services in Disadvantaged Areas.

OVERVIEW OF EXISTING TRAINING
PROVISION AND ACCREDITATION IN
THE AREA OF CHILDCARE

NCVA

The National Council for Vocational Awards was established to develop a national certification system for vocational training programmes. The NCVA structures courses on a modular basis and develops an appropriate framework of levels of qualification for courses, develops national assessment criteria, provides a certification based on trainees' performance as assessed in accordance with assessment criteria.

The work of the NCVA has led, inter alia, to the Vocational Educational Committees(VECs) strengthening and supporting a number of certificate courses in childcare leading to a National Foundation Certificate, National Vocational Certificate, Level 1 or National Vocational Certificate, Level 2.

NCEA

The National Council for Education Awards (NCEA) is the State agency responsible for co-ordination, development and promotions of higher education outside the universities. It carries out its responsibilities through the approval of courses and granting and conferring of degrees, diplomas, certificates and other educational awards.

Teastas

Teastas, the Irish National Certification Authority, was established as an interim authority to advise the Minister for Education and Science on putting in place a single, nationally and internationally accepted certification structure covering all extra-university third level and all further and continuing education and training programmes.

- The recommended national qualifications system, as set out in the Second Report of Teastas, will involve the establishment and/or recognition in legislation of:

- an appropriate Authority together with two awarding bodies and the DIT;
- clearly defined roles and functions for the Authority and the awarding bodies to ensure that they function as a single system and contribute to the National Qualifications Framework, which the Authority is to establish;
- the means whereby the Authority can have regard to the wider national context, including the establishment of effective links to other awards.

The following is an overview of existing training provision and accreditation in the area of childcare:

An Comhchoiste Reamhscolaíochta Teo

This organisation offers a basic intensive 42 hour training programme through the medium of Irish and continuous in-service courses for all Naíonra playleaders. The certificate is awarded by the organisation itself.

Barnardos

Barnardo's National Children's Resource Centre provides information and tailor made training relevant to the welfare of children in response to requests from groups and organisations. Barnardos are registered childcare trainers with FÁS.

Childminders

Courses designed specifically for childminders in Ireland are rare. Currently the NCMAI in addition to Barnardo's National Children's Resource Centre offer 10 week courses for childminders. The European Union's New Opportunities for Women (NOW) programme (see Section 1.4) have funded two projects supporting training for childminders. These were (1) 'Childcare for Tallaght', part of which was the establishment and co-ordination of a network of locally based childminders who would receive training and on-going advice and support and (2) 'Regional Family Day Care Project', which was administered by the Department of Social Policy and Social Work, University College, Dublin. The two main elements of the UCD project were a 'training of trainers' course and training of family day carers (childminders).

Dublin Institute of Technology
The Dublin Institute of Technology (DIT) offers both a Certificate (2 years) and a Diploma (3 years) in Early Childhood Care and Education. As of from 1999, DIT will be offering a 3 year Degree in Early Childhood Care and Education. All courses are validated by the DIT. As well as directly providing training to students, the DIT is actively engaged in research around the training need in the early childhood sector.

FÁS
FÁS, the National Training & Employment Authority offers the following courses in childcare: Childcare 1, a 900 hour course of 8 modules of which 360 hours are on placement; Childcare 2, a 1250 hour course of which 550 hours are on placement. The courses are certified by FÁS and successful participants are awarded a FÁS/City and Guilds Certificate. FÁS provides APL for Childcare Level 1 and Level 2. FÁS delivers its courses on a full-time and part-time basis including a flexible approach with many courses being delivered at evening and over weekends.

Irish Pre-school Playgroups Association
The Irish Pre-school Playgroups Association (IPPA) offers a range of childcare courses including the following: (1) a 20-hour Introductory playgroup course; (2) The Formative Years a 40 hour course; (3) Foundation Course, which is composed of a minimum of 90 hours tuition and 30 observation sessions; (4) Diploma in Play Group Practice; and (5) IPPA/NCVA Level 2 course which includes optional modules developed by the IPPA.

Montessori Colleges
These colleges offer training over one to three years on a part-time or full-time basis. The St. Nicholas Montessori College is an NCEA accredited college offering courses to degree level and the AMI (Association Montessori International) offer their own accreditation.

Private Colleges
Many private colleges also offer training in childcare to certificate and diploma level on a part-time or full-time basis. Most of the colleges are accredited by City and Guilds but offer their own accreditation with limited recognition.

Regional Technical Colleges
The Regional Technical Colleges offer both a National Diploma and a B.A. in Applied Social Studies in Social Care. These courses are accredited by the NCEA (National Council for Educational Awards).

University College Cork
University College Cork (UCC) offers a B.A. in Early Childhood Studies and a Certificate in Day Care Studies. Research staff in the Education Department in UCC are currently undertaking research in the area of Early Years Education with a view to developing a curriculum for the 3 to 4 year old child.

VEC Post Leaving Courses
There are approximately 27 VEC colleges throughout the country offering courses in early childhood care and education including the NCVA Level 2 in Childcare course. The course is broken into eight subject modules and is available in certain colleges on a part-time as well as a full-time basis. VEC colleges also offer and certify a one year Diploma in Montessori Education; the NNEB two year course in childcare, which is accredited by the U.K. Nursery Nurses Education Board (NNEB).

Occupational Profiles for the Childcare Sector as developed by the subgroup on Registration, Training and Qualification

Occupational Role	Key Tasks and Responsibilities
Specialist	• Training and development of personnel • Co-ordination at national and area levels • Strategic planning • Policy advice
Manager	• Overall responsibility for the operation and maintenance of the Centre/service • Provide an appropriate environment for the planning, implementing and review of programmes for the physical, emotional, cognitive development of children • Keeping all Centre accounts and records • Responsible for recruitment • Ordering supplies • Liaison with all outside agencies • Responsibility for drafting, implementing and reviewing the policies and operational procedures for the Centre • Management of personnel and team building • Ensure Centre complies with all relevant legislation • Liaising with parents
Supervisor	• Supervision and developmental support for all staff • Planning, implementing and review of all developmental programmes so as to provide for children's physical, emotional, social and cognitive development • Identifying special needs and planning for appropriate interventions either within the service provided or by other professional people • Acting as health and safety officer • Keeping children's records • Liaising with parents
Childcare Worker	• Day to day responsibility under supervision for children attending the Centre • Implementing and reviewing activities appropriate to individual and group needs so as to provide for children's physical, emotional, social and cognitive development • Observing all procedures as required in terms of care and control, safety and good childcare practice

	• Choosing, organising and maintaining equipment and materials
	• Contributing to the compiling and updating of children's records
	• Delegation of tasks to Childcare Assistants
	• Work as part of a team
	• Liaising with parents

Childcare Assistant

- Undertake routine tasks as delegated under the supervision of childcare worker/supervisor
- Maintain equipment and materials
- Contribute to the updating of children's records
- Work as part of a team
- Liaising with parents

Family Daycare (Home based)

- Provides daycare for young children in childminders own home or in a child's own home i.e. both pre-school and afterschool
- Care for children all day long for the full working week, offering a range of care and play activities like a parent at home
- Make a major contribution to children's physical, emotional, social and cognitive development.
- Liaising with parents

The above key tasks & responsibilities can also be applied in sessional services as follows:

Pre-School Leader   -   Manager/Supervisor

Pre-School Assistant   -   Childcare Worker/Assistant

Articles of the UN Convention on the Rights of the Child as referred to in this Report

The United Nations Convention on the Rights of the Child sets out the rights guaranteed to children and young people under 18 years in all areas of their lives and it imposes obligations on parents, the family, the community and the State in this regard.

Ireland signed the Convention on the Rights of the Child on 30 September, 1990 and ratified it without reservation on 21 September, 1992. This binding treaty entered into force in Ireland one month later.

Article 2

1. States Parties shall respect and ensure the rights set forth in the present Convention to each child within their jurisdiction without discrimination of any kind, irrespective of the child's or his or her parent's or legal guardian's race, colour, sex, language, religion, political or other opinion, national, ethnic or social origin, property, disability, birth or other status.

2. States Parties shall take all appropriate measures to ensure that the child is protected against all forms of discrimination or punishment on the basis of the status, activities, expressed opinions or beliefs of the child's parents, legal guardians or family members.

Article 3

1. In all actions concerning children, whether undertaken by public or private social welfare institutions, courts of law, administrative authorities or legislative bodies, the best interests of the child shall be a primary consideration.

2. States Parties undertake to ensure the child such protection and care as is necessary for his or her wellbeing, taking into account the rights and duties of his or her parents, legal guardians or other individuals legally responsible for him or her, and, to this end, shall take all appropriate legislative and administrative measures.

3. States Parties shall ensure that all institutions, services and facilities responsible for the care or protection of children shall conform with the standards established by competent authorities, particularly in the areas of safety, health, in the number and suitability of their staff as well as competent supervision.

Article 12

1. States Parties shall assure to the child who is capable of forming his or her own views the right to express those views freely in all matters affecting the child, the views of the child being given due weight in accordance with the age and maturity of the child.

2. For this purpose, the child shall in particular be provided the opportunity to be heard in any judicial and administrative proceedings affecting the child, either directly, or through a representative or an appropriate body, in a manner consistent with the procedural rules of national law.

Article 18

1. States Parties shall use their best efforts to ensure recognition of the principle that both parents have common responsibilities for the upbringing and development of the child. Parents or, as the case may be, legal guardians, have the primary responsibility for the upbringing and development of the child. The best interests of the child will be their basic concern.

2. For the purpose of guaranteeing and promoting the rights set forth in the present Convention, States Parties shall render appropriate assistance to parents and legal guardians in the performance of their child-rearing responsibilities and shall ensure the development of institutions, facilities and services for the care of children.

3. States Parties shall take all appropriate measures to ensure that children of working parents have the right to benefit from childcare services and facilities for which they are eligible.

Article 23

1. States Parties recognise that a mentally or physically disabled child should enjoy a full and decent life, in conditions which ensure dignity, promote self-reliance and facilitate the child's active participation in the community.

2. States Parties recognise the right of the disabled child to special care and shall encourage and ensure the extension, subject to available resources, to the eligible child and those responsible for his or her care, of assistance for which application is made and which is appropriate to the child's condition and to the circumstances of the parents or others caring for the child.

Article 30

In those States in which ethnic, religious or linguistic minorities or persons of indigenous origin exist, a child belonging to such a minority or who is indigenous shall not be denied the right, in community with other members of his or her group, to enjoy his or her own culture, to profess and practise his or her own religion, or to use his or her own language.

Article 31

1. States Parties recognise the right of the child to rest and leisure, to engage in play and recreational activities appropriate to the age of the child and to participate freely in cultural life and the arts.

2. States Parties shall respect and promote the right of the child to participate fully in cultural and artistic life and shall encourage the provision of appropriate and equal opportunities for cultural, artistic, recreational and leisure activity.

Benefits of Early Childhood Programmes

For	Changes in	Nature of the Change
Children	*Psycho-social Development*	Improved cognitive development (thinking, reasoning); improved social development (relationship to others); improved emotional development (self-image, security); improved language skills.
	Health and Nutrition	increased survival rates reduced morbidity, improved hygiene; improved weight/height for age; improved micronutrient balance.
	Progress and Performance in Primary School	higher chance of entering, less chance of repeating; learning and better performance.
Adults	*General Knowledge*	health and hygiene, nutrition (related to own status);
	Attitudes and Practices	leadership skills; health and hygiene, preventive medical practice, opportune treatment, nutrition: improved diet.
	Relationships	improved self-esteem, better husband-wife, parent-child, child-child relationships.
	Employment	caregivers freed to seek or improve employment, new employment opportunities created by programme, increased market for programme-related goods.
Communities	*Physical Environment*	sanitation, spaces for play, new multi-purpose facilities, improved solidarity, increased participation of women, community projects benefiting all.
Institutions	*Efficiency*	better health attention through grooming or changed user practices, reduced repetition and dropout in schools.
	Effectiveness	greater coverage
	Capacity	greater ability/confidence and/or changes in organisation, improved methods and curriculum content.
Society	*Quality of life*	a healthier population, reduced days lost to sickness, a more literate, educated population; greater social participation; an improved labour force; reduced delinquency; reduced fertility and early births; reduced social inequalities.

Source: Consultative Group on Early Childhood Care and Development Internet URL - www.ecc/group.com
Reference: report of the National Forum for Early Childhood Education (Nov 98).

ABBREVIATIONS & GLOSSARY OF TERMS

ADM Ltd Area Development Management Ltd. is an independent company designated by the Government and the EU to support integrated local economic and social development. ADM manages a range of social and economic programmes on behalf of the EU and Irish Government.

APL Accredited Prior Learnng offers an opportunity to adults to obtain credit for what they have learned in life without demanding that they return to school or college to do so. It gives credit for skills and knowledge regardless of where or how acquired and these are measured against the common standard.

Childcare Definition agreed by members of the Expert Working Group as opposed to use of term "child care" which applies to services which come under the remit of the Department of Health and Children for children considered to be in need of protection.

The term childcare is used by the Expert Working Group to describe daycare facilities and services for pre-school children and school-going children out of school hours. It includes services offering care, education and socialisation opportunities for children to the benefit of children, parents, employers and the wider community. Thus services such as pre-schools, na'onraí, daycare services, crèches, playgroups, childminding and after-school groups are included, but schools (primary, secondary and special) and residential centres for children are excluded.

The Expert Working Group also agreed that the age-group to be considered would be children aged 0 to 12 years inclusive.

Child Care Act, 1991 Legislation which updated the law in relation to the care of children, particularly children who have been assaulted, ill-treated, neglected or sexually abused or who are at risk. Part VII of the Act refers to pre-school services.

Child Care (Pre-School Services) Regulations, 1996 Regulations developed under Part VII of the Child Care Act, 1991 which require minimum standards for pre-school services and provide for providers covered by the Act to notify the Department of Health and Children of their service and to be available for inspection.

Child Individuals who provide a childcare minders service to parents in their own home or in the parent's home.

Community Employment Programme Employment programme operated by FÁS which funds sponsors to provide a work and training programme for persons who qualify for participation in the scheme. It mainly applies to persons who are over 21 years, unemployed and in receipt of a qualifying social welfare payment for a period of at least one year.

CEB City and County Enterprise Boards (CEBs) were established in October, 1993 under one of three sub-programmes of the EU Operational Programme for Local Urban and Rural Development, 1994 to 1999 (part of the CSF 1994-1999). The Boards are locally controlled development companies set up to develop indigenous enterprise potential and to stimulate economic activity at local level by providing funding for the development of micro enterprise. The Department of Enterpise, Trade and Employment has administrative responsibility for the sub-programme.

Commission on the Family The Commission on the Family was established by the Minister for Social Welfare in 1995 to examine the effects of legislation and policies on families and make recommendations to the Government on proposals which would strengthen the capacity of families to carry out their functions in a changing environment. The Commission published a report in July, 1998.

CSER Centre for Social and Educational Research based in the Dublin Institute of Technology.

CSF Community Support Framework.

DIT Dublin Institute of Technology.

DIT/ NOW Early Childhood Project supported by the EU EMPLOYMENT/NOW fund which was set up at the end of 1995 to establish a mutually recognised system of accreditation for early childhood care and education and to develop APL as a means of doing this. The project is backed by a consultative group representing the major accrediting, training and practitioner bodies in the relevant areas throughout Ireland.

Early Start Programme This programme is operated by the Department of Education and Science for children aged 3 years and over in disadvantaged communities covering 40 primary schools. It provides a one year pre-primary school programme to participants.

EC Childcare Network The EC Childcare Network was established by the EC Commission's Equal Opportunities Unit in 1986 under the second Action Programme. It published a series of reports on specific issues concerning services for young children, including: family daycare services, services providing care and recreation for school-age children, the childcare needs of rural families, information for monitoring services and the costs of funding services.

Equal Opportunities Childcare Programme The Department of Justice, Equality and Law Reform provides funding for the development of childcare under the Equal Opportunities Childcare Programme which is administered by ADM Ltd. The Programme is designed to support local communities in disadvantaged areas and employers who wish to assist employees to reconcile work and family commitments. It provides funding under 3 initiatives:
- Capital Infrastructure funding for community projects in disadvantaged areas;
- Core funding to 25 community projects nationwide;
- Employer Demonstration Initiative which is led by IBEC.

ERDF European Regional Development Fund provides funding mainly to capital projects. Assistance focuses primarily on productive investments, the creation or modernisation of infrastructure, as well as investment in education and health.

ESF   European Social Fund concentrates on developing human resources aiming to tackle unemployment, through the creation of new job opportunities and supporting the development of skills and qualifications.

ESRI   Economic and Social Research Institute

EU   European Union

Family   Refers to childminding services.
Daycare

FÁS   National Training and Employment Authority whose functions include the operation of training and employment programmes and support for co-operative and community-based enterprise. FÁS operates under the aegis of the Department of Enterprise, Trade and Employment.

Health   The Health Act, 1970 provided
Boards   for the establishment of eight health boards which have been responsible for the administration of health services in Ireland since April, 1971. They are responsible for a number of programmes including community care services.

High/   Refers to an approach to early
Scope   childhood care and education
Project   which has been shaped and developed by research over a thirty year period. The High/Scope Model Curriculum has been researched in the USA in longitudinal studies

evaluating the outcome of quality early childhood education services on a control group of disadvantaged children. Outcome was assessed when the group of participants had reached age 27 years. A cost benefit analysis revealed that for every $1 invested in each child there was a return of $7 to the public due to reduced crime, increased educational performance, economic status and commitment to marriage.

Human   Human Resources Operational
Resources   Programme concentrates on the
OP   development of human resources in Ireland investing in the training and upskilling of the workforce or those who wish to access the workforce. The programme receives funding from the ESF and ERDF. 80% of ESF aid to Ireland is channelled through this programme.

IBEC   Irish Business and Employers' Confederation

ICTU   Irish Congress of Trade Unions.

IMEB   Irish Montessori Education Board

IPPA   Irish Pre-Schools and Playgroups Association

Joint   The Labour Court is empowered
Labour   to establish a Joint Labour
Committee   Committee (JLC) under the Industrial Relations Act, 1946. JLCs consist of equal numbers of representatives of employers and workers appointed by the Labour Court and a Chair and independent member appointed by the Minister for Enterprise, Trade and Employment. An application for the establishment of a JLC must be on the grounds that there is

substantial agreement between the workers and employers or that existing machinery for the effective regulation of wages and conditions for employment of the workers concerned is inadequate, or that having regard to existing rates of remuneration and conditions that it is expedient that a JLC should be established.

LEADER   An EU Community Initiative for rural development which is based on a "bottom-up" concept of development and provides rural communities with opportunities to involve themselves directly in the development of their own areas. 34 local groups have been approved to implement their business plans during the period of the programme. The Department of Agriculture and Food is responsible for overseeing the programme in Ireland.

Naíonraí   Irish language medium playgroups offering sessional services for children age 3 to 5 years.

National Anti-Poverty Strategy   The National Anti-Poverty Strategy (NAPS) was launched in April 1997 with the overall objective of reducing the proportion of the population living in poverty from 9-15% to less than 5-10% by the year 2007. The NAPS was designed on the basis of 5 key themes - unemployment, educational disadvantage, income adequacy, disadvantaged urban areas and rural poverty - each with its own set of targets and timeframes. A NAPS strategic management inititative unit has been established in the Department of Social, Community and

Family Affairs to help co-ordinate and develop cross-departmental action to support social inclusion and anti-poverty measures.

NCMAI   National Childminding Association of Ireland

NCNA   National Children's Nurseries Association.

National Forum for Early Childhood Education   This Forum was convened by the Minister for Education and Science in early 1998, in recognition of the significance of quality education within a lifelong educational framework. The focus of the Forum was on children aged 0 to 6 years. The Forum invited submissions and presentations from relevant organisations and following discussion and analysis a report was published by the Secretariat on the 10 November, 1998.

NWCI   National Women's Council of Ireland.

NESC   National Economic and Social Council.

NOW   New Opportunities for Women Programme funded by the EU Employment Initiative. It aims to reduce female unemployment and increase opportunities in the labour market for women.

Partnership 2000   National Agreement for Inclusion, Employment and Competiveness 1997-2000 agreed by the Government and social partners. An important new development in the negotiations leading to the agreement was the involvement of the community and voluntary sector as the fourth pillar.

Pilot Childcare Initiative   This was an initiative by the Department of Equality and Law Reform which operated for the period 1994 to 1997 providing funding for the development of childcare services in disadvantaged areas to enable women (and men where they have responsibility for rearing their young children) to avail of education, training and employment opportunities which they would otherwise be unable to do in the absence of childcare facilities. The programme was administered through ADM Ltd.

Pre-School Services   Childcare services for children aged 3 - 6 years.

P & R Programme   EU Special Support Programme for Peace & Reconciliation which provides funding to projects in the counties on either side of the Northern Ireland Border under a number of programmes covering employment, urban and rural regeneration, social inclusion (covers childcare also) and productive investment. ADM Ltd and the Combat Poverty Agency have responsibility for jointly administering the funding which was allocated to the six southern border counties.

PRSI   Pay Related Social Insurance.

RTC   Regional Technical College

Sessional Services   Services provided for a limited number of hours per day e.g. pre-school and playgroup services which normally operate for a number of hours in the mornings.

VEC   Vocational Education Committees provide and manage vocational schools, employ managerial and teaching staff and provide vocational and continuation education. Activities are financed partly from local rates and partly from State grants.

VTOS   Vocational Training Opportunities Scheme is a special range of courses designed to meet the education and training needs of unemployed people. VTOS is funded by the Department of Education and Science, with assistance from the ESF.

Youthreach   Training and education programme for early school leavers who are age 15 to 18 years. The programme receives EU funding via the Department of Education and Science and is managed by the VECs nationwide.